1979

AUSTRIAN LIFE AND LITERATURE 1780-1938

AUSTRIAN LIFE
AND LITERATURE
1780-1938

Eight Essays

EDITED BY

PETER BRANSCOMBE

SCOTTISH ACADEMIC PRESS

EDINBURGH

1978

Reprinted from
FORUM FOR MODERN LANGUAGE STUDIES
Volume XIII No. 2

———

Published by
Scottish Academic Press Ltd.
33 Montgomery Street, Edinburgh 7

SBN 7073 0144 0

This edition first published 1978

Printed in Great Britain by
W. C. Henderson & Son Ltd., St. Andrews

FOREWORD

This collection of eight essays covers aspects of Austrian life and literature from the age of Joseph II to the end of the First Republic. No attempt has been made—or indeed could be made, in eight short essays—to cover every author of importance, or even every literary form. Instead, the editor invited colleagues to write articles on subjects of their own choosing, confident that what they wrote would throw new light on comparatively familiar subjects, or focus attention on unjustly neglected themes and authors.

Peter Horwath draws attention to a forgotten but once very popular Austrian novel which clearly shows that Richardson's influence extended to late 18th-century Vienna; W. E. Yates examines the realities behind the myth of a Golden Age of Viennese culture in the early 19th century, using much unfamiliar material and looking critically at a number of hallowed but misleading assumptions. W. N. B. Mullan considers Grillparzer's links with tradition in the light of the dramatist's own pronouncements, and weighs the varying claims of those who would align Grillparzer with the main developments in 19th-century German literature. Viennese *Vormärz* writers are also the subjects chosen for study by P. M. Potter (a reappraisal of a Nestroy play which has provided problems for the categorists and embarrassment for detractors unable to account for its great success), and Peter Branscombe (an analysis of Stifter's use of Leitmotifs in *Brigitta* based on a comparison between the original published text and its later revision).

L. H. Bailey considers two 19th-century Viennese writers who are unfairly dismissed as mere journalists; their short essays have outlived the *feuilleton* section of the papers for which they were written and emerge as sensitive, witty and penetrating comments on the preoccupations of the Viennese in the second half of the 19th century. M. A. Rogers takes an aphorism by Hebbel (Viennese by adoption before rejection) as the starting-point for his examination of the validity of claims about the Austrianness of Austrian literature, comparing aspects of Nestroy's art with that of his successor Karl Kraus. Finally, A. F. Bance analyses a Horváth play which, despite its Bavarian setting and its author's Hungarian provenance, reveals the continuing vitality of the Austrian *Volksstück* tradition and its appropriateness for a statement on the cultural and economic crises of the inter-war years.

Disparate the subject-matter of these studies may be, but the authors they examine and the literary and cultural concerns they evince are typical of the recurring preoccupations of Austria's writers and public alike. Vienna's old-world charm may well be mythical, but like all myths it is based on incontrovertible facts; these essays focus attention on some of the most persistent of them.

P. J. B.

(v)

CONTRIBUTORS

PETER HORWATH is Professor of German at Arizona State University, where he has taught since 1973. His research interests lie mainly in Austrian and German literary and sociological studies, and his book *Der Kampf gegen die religiöse Tradition: Die Kulturkampfliteratur Österreichs, 1780-1918*, is in the press.

W. E. YATES taught at the University of Durham before being appointed to the Chair of German at Exeter in 1972. He has edited plays by Hofmannsthal and Grillparzer, and is the author of monographs on Grillparzer and Nestroy and of numerous articles on Austrian literature and theatre of the 19th and 20th centuries.

W. N. B. MULLAN has been a Lecturer in German at St Andrews since 1969, having studied at Trinity College Dublin and at Oxford. He is the author of a B.Litt. thesis on Grillparzer's aesthetic theory, and is currently pursuing his researches into the relationship between theory and practice in the works of Grillparzer.

P. M. POTTER studied at the University College of Swansea, in Vienna, and at the University of British Columbia. Since 1974 he has been a Lecturer in German at the University of Ife, Nigeria. Apart from his continuing interest in Nestroy and the Viennese popular theatre tradition, he is engaged in doctoral research on Ödön von Horváth.

PETER BRANSCOMBE has taught at St Andrews since 1959. His research interests are divided between Austrian literature (especially the Viennese *Volkstheater*), musicology (18th and 19th centuries), and Heine. He is co-editor of a volume of international Schubert studies to be published by the Cambridge University Press to mark the 150th anniversary of Schubert's death.

L. H. BAILEY studied at the Universities of Oxford and Cambridge (where he wrote a doctoral thesis on the *Wiener Skizze*) and has taught at the Universities of St Andrews (1972-74) and Vienna (since 1974). He is continuing his researches into the Viennese 19th-century *Feuilleton*.

M. A. ROGERS studied at Cambridge and in Vienna, and since 1972 has been a Lecturer in German at the University of Southampton. He wrote his Cambridge doctoral thesis on "Elements of Convention and Theatricality in the Works of Johann Nestroy", and is currently working on Karl Kraus and Trakl.

A. F. BANCE studied at the Universities of London and Cambridge (where he wrote a doctoral thesis on the German novel since 1945). After a year as Lektor at Graz and an appointment at Strathclyde University he took up his present post as Lecturer in German at St Andrews in 1967. His publications include articles on Thomas Mann, Fontane and Remarque, and an edition of Joseph Roth's *Radetzkymarsch*.

CONTENTS

I

RICHARDSONIAN CHARACTERS AND MOTIFS IN JOHANN FRIEDEL'S NOVEL *ELEONORE*

As in England, Richardson's novels easily and quickly won the hearts of the German middle class.[1] *Pamela* (1740-41) appeared in German translation in 1743; *Clarissa* (1747-48) appeared between 1748 and 1751, and requests for sheets for *Sir Charles Grandison* (1753-54) came from Germany even as the novel was being printed, so that a German edition could appear in 1754-55.[2] In Germany, where a veritable *Grandisonfieber* raged, Richardson was placed by such persons as Gellert above Homer. The Englishman's works influenced those of J. E. Schlegel, C. F. Gellert, G. E. Lessing, C. M. Wieland, J. T. Hermes, J. M. Miller, S. von La Roche, A. von Knigge, W. Heinse, F. H. Jacobi, R. Lenz, and J. W. von Goethe.[3] However, Richardson did not only find admirers and imitators, but also parodists and scoffers (J. K. Musäus, F. Nicolai). Musäus' parody *Grandison der Zweite oder Geschichte des Herrn v. N*** in Briefen entworfen* (1760-62) was the first German novel in letters.

Although Richardson's novels had a most profound influence on the development of the German novel, it is quite startling to realize that Austria seems to have been bypassed. The monumental *Deutsch-Österreichische Literaturgeschichte* (1899-1937) edited by J. W. Nagl, J. Zeidler and E. Castle mentions Richardson only once in its 4309 pages, and that in regard to J. B. von Alxinger's epic poem *Bliomberis* (1791). And yet, there was in the person of Johann Friedel (1751? 1752? 1755?-89) from Temeschburg in the Banat a second Austrian who under the influence of Richardson's novels produced a novel in letters, *Eleonore: Kein Roman: Eine wahre Geschichte in*

Briefen (2 vols., Berlin u. Leipzig: G. J. Decker, 1780-81), which was destined to become an immediate international bestseller, being translated, e.g. into Dutch (1788) and Italian, and to see several editions (1780; 1781; 1788).[4]

Notwithstanding his untimely death, Friedel was one of the most influential literary figures of the Austrian Enlightenment under Joseph II. On his death he left behind a corpus of writings which is still today of value to the ethnographer and cultural historian. His many-faceted *Briefe verschiedenen Inhalts* . . . (1784)[5] about Berlin and Vienna were European sensations, and a thorn in the flesh of the Prussian critic and writer F. Nicolai. Friedel also achieved a dubious fame as a plagiarist. While still a soldier he seems to have enjoyed the protection of his military superior, the poet Ayrenhoff. Toward the end of 1783 Friedel joined Schikaneder's touring group as an actor. In 1785 he became the lover of Schikaneder's wife Eleonore, with whom he founded a theatre company, and in 1788-89 he directed the Theater auf der Wieden. After Friedel's death in the same year Schikaneder, the future librettist of the *Magic Flute*, took over Friedel's vacant post.

Friedel's talents were largely of a journalistic, and less of a poetic and literary, nature. Making ends meet was one of the motivating forces for his literary activities; another was his zeal for social and ecclesiastical reforms. Nevertheless, the *Wiener Kirchenzeitung* did not refrain from praising one of Austria's first "Jacobins" and a champion of Josephinism for his company's frequent performances on behalf of the poor. Around 1777 the youthful Friedel had ventured into the field of drama with his tragedy *Norwich und Julie* (1778 pirated edition; 1785 Friedel's edition). Not unlike Richardson, Friedel shows here a marked preference for contrasting scenes of sentimentality and brutality.[6] In the Richardsonian tradition are the motifs of the rake and virtue in distress. But it was in his novel *Eleonore* a few years later that Friedel most determinedly ploughed with Richardson's heifer.

The author claims to have been in one of the most elegant capitals of Germany at a time when a strange catastrophe was setting in. To narrate the events, which the author claims to have witnessed, he produces 88 letters (6 January 1773-3 August 1774) from the pen of 11 correspondents in the unfolding drama.

Countess Eleonore is by ducal command enjoined to marry the hedonistic young Count Flett. The Court expects that the unsurpassed virtue of Eleonore will cause Flett to reform. Flett, however, departs immediately after the wedding for Paris where he engages in numerous gallant adventures. He not only seduces the wife of his middle class friend Desnier, but he also challenges the hapless man to a duel. Desnier's guilt-ridden wife becomes insane and dies. Everyone forgives her ("Die Sinne sind nicht das Herz", I, 73). Flett is forced to flee to Spaa, a watering place in Belgium.

Even though Flett has been away now for over a year, Eleonore slowly falls in love with her absent husband. She believes Flett would have remained virtuous had he not been forced into marriage. The fate of the

Desniers did indeed affect Flett's moral sensibility but the unsavory influence of a certain Captain Blau takes him off the path of virtue. The high-principled Baron Hart had expended much energy in an attempt to reform Flett. Hart gets to know Eleonore and they come to respect each other highly.

Flett's next victim is Louise, the innocent daughter of an innkeeper. An Italian adventurer, the Abbate Veronese, succeeds in obtaining the girl for him through trickery and misrepresentation. A mock marriage takes place in which one of Veronese's helpmates, an Italian bandit, plays the role of priest. When Louise finds out the true marital status of Flett, Flett promises to divorce Eleonore and marry her. He is genuinely enamoured with Louise.

To ruin Eleonore, Veronese sets out to awaken in her a love for Hart, and he succeeds. Eleonore and Hart decide to flee. In their flight they are surprised by Veronese's bandits, and Hart seems to have been killed in the attack. All guilt seems now to fall on Eleonore. In the eyes of the court Flett seems to be innocent. Flett asks for permission to divorce Eleonore but he no longer intends to marry Louise. Eleonore and Louise happen to end up in the same convent, but Louise, showing signs of pregnancy, is mercilessly turned out.

In the meantime, Batt, Louise's former lover, has stumbled upon the wounded Hart and nursed him back to life. Batt also discovers Louise and forgives her. Eleonore learns of Hart's survival.

Flett receives orders to return to Germany to explain his connections with Veronese's bandits. Veronese, it turns out, is not an abbate at all but a multiple killer. One of his most hideous crimes was the poisoning of the parents and sister of the Parmesan Count L** ("Richardsons realisierter Grandison", II, 105). Count L** is in search of Veronese. Flett hypocritically plans to blame Veronese for all the evil doings.

The Court asks Eleonore to return to her husband but she is in love with Hart and in her renewed despair she takes refuge in a convent. Louise's fate had been a cruel one: first she was lured into a brothel and then arrested for vagrancy. Batt obtains her release from jail and the two marry. Veronese, having seen through Flett's intentions, has him seriously wounded, and to prevent him from talking he cuts out his tongue. Before dying, Flett repents. Veronese is apprehended. Sent to jail, he commits suicide by swallowing broken glass. Eleonore and Hart marry; so do Count L** and Eleonore's confidante Fräulein Julchen.

While the general public savoured the novel's pathos and sensuality, Friedel's enemy in Berlin, Christoph Friedrich Nicolai, sharply criticized it in his *Allgemeine Deutsche Bibliothek*: "Wenn sie [die handelnden Figuren] würklich möglich wären, wie wir doch zu Ehren der Menschheit leugnen, worzu soll denn ein so abscheuliches Gemählde; Etwan taumelnden Wollüstlern Gründe zu ihren Handlungen und Verblendungen zu leihen? . . . Wehe dem Schriftsteller, welcher auch nur einen Menschen unglücklich macht;"[7] It is quite understandable that a journal dedicated to the spread of an asensual rationalism and the development of a higher type of man should have found a rogue à la Flett vexing. Shocking must also have been the scene which describes the Abbate's rape of the dying Sophie, the sister of Count L**:

> Aber der Anblick, den der unvermeidliche Tod seiner Geliebten ihm verursachen mußte, setzte ihn in Raserei: Er ließ die Kutsche halten, hob sie heraus, und—da er an dem Genusse seiner Begierde wegen ihres nahen Todes auf die Zukunft verzweifelte, so benutzte er die Schwäche des mit dem Tode ringenden Mädchens und—Gott, meine Hand bebt, und sträubt sich die Schandthat dieses Teufels—auszuschreiben. Er warf die zween Kavaliere neben sich hin, und ließ Sophie geschändet liegen. (II, 100)

Nicolai's criticism is somewhat narrowly rationalistic and moralistic, and Friedel in his scornful reply[8] understandably objects to the biased, undetailed and sanctimonious nature of Nicolai's review. Friedel's *Eleonore* has a greater literary merit than both Nicolai and later G. Gugitz are willing to grant, and this fact should become evident in the following attempt at indicating Richardsonian characters, topics, and motifs. Yet, before embarking on this task it might be rewarding to speculate whether Friedel had a specific German capital in mind and whether *Eleonore* also responds to certain concrete situations of Friedel's time. For it seems that Friedel's Rousseauesque criticism of absolutism's interference in man's most private sphere is more than a useful motif around which to weave a tale that at times strains credulity.

Friedel, one recalls, places the action in the later years of the reign of Maria Theresia, to be precise 1773-74. It is indeed a sort of Austrian Caesaropapist Catholic state that Friedel describes. In this state the "Fürstin" exercises power even within the *ius circa sacra* (e.g. ordering the Bishop to have Eleonora committed to a convent). Lecturing Flett on civil disobedience, Pastor Hamoniens of "Hamburg"[9] expresses sentiments that echo views of the Josephinist Austrian theologian Franz X. Gmeiner. Pastor Hamoniens categorically states: "Man kann dem Staat nie ungehorsam seyn, ohne es auch gegen den Willen des Höchsten zu seyn. Indem Sie sich also wider den ausdrücklichen Willen Ihres Fürsten sträuben, sträuben Sie sich auch wider den geheimen Willen Ihres Schöpfers" (II, 125).[10] These and the following considerations seem to indicate quite clearly that Friedel's "Fürstin" is the Empress Maria Theresia and the capital city referred to, Vienna. Friedel, having to worry continuously about finances, could have had a very good reason for naming his heroine Eleonore, for this name was quite well known to the Viennese. It was Austria's foremost reformer Freiherr Joseph von Sonnenfels (1741-1805) who, in order to educate and emancipate the Austrian female properly, had started in 1767 a weekly, *Theresia und Eleonore*. Two years before this venture the Empress had suppressed his weekly *Der Mann ohne Vorurteil*, and it seems plausible that Sonnenfels, wanting to retain or to regain his sovereign's good will, included the Empress' name in the title. Now, if Friedel did have Sonnenfels' weekly and its intentions in mind, then the "Fürstin" could be equated with Maria Theresia, and the aspirations of his Eleonore with the Eleonore of Sonnenfels. This theory gains some additional support from the fact that Friedel wrote an "Ode auf das Namensfest Maria Theresias" (1775) and that his "Fürst" plays an exceedingly minor role, apparently concerned primarily with foreign policy. Historical authority shows that in 1773-74 Joseph II was already co-regent and that his concerns were those of conducting the external affairs of the Empire.

Eleonore contains several passages that reflect the anti-monastic temper of Austria's antipapalists, puritanic Reform Catholics and Atheists of the 1770s and '80s. The same premises seem to be partially responsible for the humorous passages *à la Hanswurst* dealing with reliquaries and visitations by the Papal Nuncio who, as father confessor, obtains valuable information from his credulous and unsuspecting aristocratic penitents.

A detailed examination of *Eleonore* might reveal to what extent Friedel's novel is Richardsonian—either through a personal acquaintance with the English writer's novels or through the Richardsonian tradition. In spite of the reference to Grandison, even a cursory reading will reveal that Friedel's novel shows a greater resemblance to *Clarissa* than to *Grandison*. However, there is one essential difference in the aims of the two authors. While Richardson invents his characters and their fate to instruct and to inspire, Friedel invents actions and characters primarily to entertain and to affect the reader's emotions. Whereas Richardson teaches his readers what virtue is, and what it takes to be a good Christian, Friedel's characters already know whether they themselves lead a Christian life or not. Maxims, reflections, and sentiments are essential to Richardson's picture of manners.[11] His letters are vehicles of edification and instruction;[12] they are realistic vignettes and peepholes into the world of debauchers, the mercantile middle class, and the fascinating aristocrats (who behave the way the middle class believed them to behave). In Austria, the middle class was still pre-mercantile, hiding its savings in stockings in the mattress of the bed. The emerging banking class was viewed with some distrust, perhaps envy. Moreover, the mercantile middle class of England was far more fascinating to write about than Austria's class, say, of apothecaries and the like. Friedel, besides lacking the talent, interest, and time for sharp observation, is mainly concerned with the emotional and psychological states of his characters, and here he uses his letter-writing skill with considerable success. As a matter of fact, this skill is his supreme achievement. On the other hand, his talent for inventing plausible plots is downright mediocre. In terms of their epistolary style, with both authors the letters rise, though much less with Friedel, to the level of dramatic confessional literature. Richardson tends to shock in order to warn; Friedel seems to shock because, like other Josephinists, he delights in doing so, and because of a certain hatred (on the part of the poor actor-writer?) for the successful upper middle class financier. Both writers seem to maintain a certain ambiguous relationship to sexuality, and this suppressed sexuality may also be responsible for the shock quality of certain passages.

Friedel's German contemporaries considered pessimism and suicidal inclinations to be an English malady. Pamela contemplates suicide and overcomes this temptation as a Christian. Hart, too, is tempted to end his life, and here, through Batt, is the novel's only explicit reference to matters "Christian": the proper attitude of a Christian. The problem of filial duty is resolved in *Eleonore* by establishing a bond of friendship between mother and daughter which no outside factor can destroy. Richardson rejects the view that filial duty is an absolute article of faith (*Grandison*). Friedel states quite explicitly that no woman can be forced to marry someone else even if this person be "ein rechtschaffener Mann" (II, 191). Richardson's mild nationalistic stance derives from the desire to calm the sensibilities of his insular readers. Friedel refers to Paris as a wicked city and pokes fun at perfumed and lisping French dandies, but he is clearly worried that the Fletts would give the Germans a bad name in France. Both authors are capable of presenting foreigners as noble and good.

Bearing in mind that Richardson is concerned in great detail with every important facet of middle-class and upper-class English life, whereas Friedel's concerns are few—love as a precondition of marriage; misuse of a person's (sacrificial) love and trust; and the right to passion—one is nevertheless startled by a series of parallels in regard to character, topic, and motif. The following of Friedel's major topics are also present in Richardson's works: (1) The suffering of the innocent, (2) the illusion of reforming a rake, (3) the nature of a good man (regardless of social status), (4) the relationship between parent and daughter, (5) the relationship between man and woman, and (6) self-sacrificing, deceived, and fallen virtue. Essentially, Friedel is concerned with the limits of a monarch's power in the sphere of a person's most intimate private life, and with a person's quite normal need to love, to be loved, and to be passionate. Certain minor aspects have approximations in Richardson's novels: (1) The nature and effect of seduction, (2) the problem of social stratification and intermarriage, (3) the rogue abroad, (4) the egocentricity and sexual depravity of the affluent upper-middle class, (5) friendship, (6) suicide, and (7) convents.

There are also a number of motifs that bear considerable resemblance towards each other: Richardson's sham marriage (*Pamela, Grandison*) finds its equivalent in the bandit who pretends he is a priest; the Brescian bravos (*Grandison*) find their counterparts in Abbate Veronese's Italian bandits, and Grandison's intrepidity in the face of marauding Croatian pandours is akin to Batt's courage upon facing the sinister bandits. The doping and subsequent raping of Clarissa has a gory Gothic parallel in Veronese's rape of Countess Sophie. Whereas Lovelace jestingly threatens his confidant Belford with cutting his throat for knowing too much, Friedel's Abbate indeed does cut out Flett's tongue for similar reasons. Clarissa is expected to marry the base Solmes; Eleonore is forced to marry the debauched Flett. Clarissa must prove her virtue in every situation (in prison, in the brothel, in grief, and in despair); similar demands are made of Friedel's heroines. A Mrs Jewkes (*Pamela*) or a Mrs Sinclair (*Clarissa*) have their crude counterparts in the brothel-keeper of *Eleonore*. Not unlike Clarissa, Louise is sent to jail upon leaving the brothel.

Richardson's heroes are quite reflective; Friedel's are not. Richardson's main characters are full of psychological paradoxes. A lover such as Lovelace has indeed more complexes than the classical Don Juan,[13] whose type of love is in its source and fulfilment the enemy of love; a heroine of the type of Clarissa is incapable of love because she is incapable of giving and receiving passion and taking risks, and thus beyond the bounds of sexual and emotional temptation and human imperfection. Friedel's characters are simple and basic; only of Eleonore does one wonder why this woman is so unconvincingly willing to prostrate herself so much. Psychologically convincing is Eleonore's slowly falling in love with Hart after her confession.

The social, filial and private demands of the Richardsonian world give rise to the "divided self": the dutiful daughter who cannot obey and the lover who must experience revenge. This phenomenon is also present in Eleonore. Both authors betray a fine insight into the female psyche, and both, while retaining the traditional male unchanged, present in Pamela, Clarissa, and to a considerable extent in Eleonore, "new women". Already Milton observed that "nunneries" no longer provided "convenient stowage for withered daughters".[14] Owing to the absence of monasticism, a young (middle class) woman in Protestant countries was under great pressure to get married—love or not. Self-support being out of the question, matrimony became the pivot for a woman, for middle class prosperity was rarely adequate for the task of supporting the livelihood of a spinster. This fact combined with other considerations gave the parents absolute control over the marital destiny of their daughters. Clarissa, even though haste, trickery, and treachery were involved, removed herself from the jurisdiction of her father and risked facing the outside world all by herself and on her own terms. Friedel's Eleonore, too, rebels. But she has the assurance that she can take refuge in a convent should her venture fail. Moreover, she enjoys the friendship of her mother, which Clarissa does not. Here a similar "Lebensgefühl" exists to that in Mme de Lafayette's *La Princesse de Clèves* (1678), where, in the face of "impossible love", a young woman retreats to a convent. Friedel seems to go beyond the concerns of Richardson by asking in the spirit of Rousseau and of the *Sturm und Drang* the radically new question whether the fact that a man is honest will be sufficient reason for insisting that a girl marry him (II, 191). Generally speaking, Friedel's women, in the face of the slow change in social stratification and values in Austria, come to terms with their lot in life. While Pamela marries into a different social class, Louise, reflecting on her sham marriage with Flett, comes to realize that there is no sense in loving someone whose station in life is so different from hers.[15] Richardson's women are set (partially because they are embodiments of principles and rules). Their virtue resides, so to speak, in their unbending will. They hold out, even when the consequences signify despondency, suicide, madness. They do not respond to flattery. As a matter of fact they abhor flattery, and they do not let themselves be seduced. Only Pamela seems to daydream about seduction. They never feel uncomfortable or guilty because of their refusal to respond to the needs and nature of their male counterparts. Friedel's women, on the other hand, are "weak" as females, and a distinction is made between the senses and the heart. (Eleonore appears under the motto: "Wer kann aufrecht bleiben, wenn eine solche Tugend fällt," I, 259). They respond to flattery, to the romantic or evil lover, and to the satisfaction of social climbing. They reflect their sexuality in their tears and sighs; and, in their insecurity and naiveté, they can feel themselves (as in the case of Eleonore) responsible for a man's debauchery. As a matter of fact, they would even accept a rogue for a husband, because their female instincts tell them that they can reform him. From Rousseau they seem to have learned to verbalize their longings and passions, and when they surrender, they surrender unconditionally.

Friedel's good persons have very much in common with each other. There is actually little individuality to them, and this fact is reflected also in their soulful diction, inspired by Klopstock and Rousseau. The rogues Flett and Blau are committed to a diction somewhat reminiscent of the pathos of *Sturm und Drang*.

"Nature" devoid of virtue and high sentiment signifies sexuality which bestows pleasure and involves a succession of faceless "Nymphe[n]" (II, 43). "Nature" in a higher sense causes a joyous relationship between man and woman in whose lives the sexual passion fuses with emotional and spiritual needs and aspirations. The misdirection of one's talents and gifts (as with the Abbate Veronese) leads to total depravity, and as with Richardson, virtue is rewarded and vice punished. Friedel's concept of virtue outside the realm of sexuality smacks somewhat of the utilitarianism of the Enlightenment. Richardson's perfect man Sir Charles Grandison remains a fascinating (though unchanging) character because of his great intellectual capacity, and not because of his near-perfection. Friedel's Count L**[16] and Hart are uninteresting because they have nothing to offer intellectually and experientially. As for rakes, Richardson's Pollexfen and Friedel's Flett are "rogues". But Pollexfen is forceful and imaginative, and Flett is weak and colourless. Both Lovelace and Flett subscribe to the motto that variety is everything, but Lovelace is considerate to his many "loves" and probably quite selective in his "nymphs" (II, 398; Friedel uses the same word), and in addition he is a good landlord. Both are on occasion capable of true remorse and deep emotions, and perhaps even of love. Flett, like Lovelace and Sir Pollexfen, exposes himself to gallant temptations in France. And what Richardson maintains of rakes, namely that even they love modest women, holds true also for Friedel. Like Mr. B.——, Flett finds girls from ranks beneath him more natural and genuine than those of his own class. Richardson's most sinister character, the sordid Tomlinson, is a relatively harmless person compared with Flett's helpmate, the Abbate.

Even when Richardson does not approve of a certain course of action, he remains calm. While Friedel's language is mellifluous, it often conveys baroque ecstacy ("Engel vom Weib", I, 83) combined with the new pathos found in Klopstock and Rousseau. Whereas Richardson's key phrases are "virtue", "merit", "duty", Friedel relies on "Tugend", "würdig sein/ machen", "Wollust", "Natur", and "Liebe". Friedel's heroines do faint, but not in moments when their chastity is endangered. The action-sequences of *Eleonore* are often picaresque (the Abbate Veronese and his bandits on their "ecclesiastical" trip to Poland) and Gothic in the manner of the *Schauer- und Räubberromane*. Both authors keep their readers' minds fluctuating between hope and despair by increasing or decreasing the speed of action. Richardson employs meaningful images and even names (Lovelace=loveless). What Friedel's strange names may signify is beyond conjecture unless one sees in Flett a word conceived in the manner of Fielding and Hermes and derived from "unflätig".

Eleonore seems to reflect Friedel's ambiguous attitude toward essentials of religious belief. It seems that he rejects the concept of God as a merciful Father (II, 151). Apparently he does not subscribe to the (inappropriately stated) idea that "unschuldig leiden, ist das größte Glück, daß dem Sterblichen zu Theil werden kann" (I, 21). There is a view expressed whereby an individual's life is a link in the chain of the nature of God, this chain holding everything together. He who implores God to end his sufferings by terminating his life commits religious treason because he is willing to break this chain. In its first part this statement is akin to Diderot's speculations.

There is little social criticism in *Eleonore*. In view of Friedel's later literary polemics one reason for this may be found in the fact that this novel was written before 1781—the year in which Joseph II greatly increased the freedom of the press. Friedel is bothered by the aristocracy's "Mätressenwirtschaft", which is supposed to have had its inception during the wars with the French, and which is even tolerated by the church provided one showed respect to the "Hw. Schmerbauch" and "dickwanstige Herrn Prälaten" (II, 139) and their "Schnickschnack" (II, 140).

All in all, Friedel's novel definitely reflects a strong indebtedness to Richardson and to the Richardsonian tradition (perhaps S. La Roche's *Geschichte des Fräuleins von Sternheim*) in Germany. Despite the absence of any conclusive proof, I believe that Friedel knew Richardson's novels.

Friedel's rogue Flett seems to have been created under the impression of Lovelace. Eleonore is almost unthinkable without a prior acquaintance with Clarissa. And themes from all three of Richardson's novels are present in Friedel's work. The fact that *Eleonore* was an international bestseller does not mean that it is aesthetically and intellectually on a par with Richardson's novels. However, as my analysis shows, *Eleonore* is more than just a "besserer Räuberroman",[17] especially in respect of technique.

In conclusion it may be appropriate to consider the question as to why Richardson's works exerted so little influence on Austrian literature. By and large Austrians prefer to be entertained rather than preached to. Moreover, the pre-1780 Austrian middle class was still healthily religious in a baroque-Catholic sense and did not need—as was the case with Protestant Germany—fictitious "saints" which Clarissa and Grandison clearly are (cf. the psychology behind the "beautiful soul" concept of Protestant German literature). That Friedel's Hart and Count L** are such pale figures is to a large extent due to the fact that neither Friedel nor his audience had as yet an inner need for an ideal secular man created by fiction. Within a short time, when in the wake of the intense anti-religious propaganda saints and wonders became unfashionable for the secularized segment of the rationalist middle class (largely represented by the bureaucracy), literature produced the prototype of a noble person in the form of Johann Pezzl's (1756-1823) Faustin (*Faustin, oder das philosophische Jahrhundert*, 1783) as an "ersatz"-saint. Thus a subconscious need was taken care of. The world of mystery, which was driven out of the churches and which the rationalists no longer wished to experience in these sacred precincts, reappeared in Schikaneder's *Magic Flute* (presented on 30 September 1791 with Schikaneder in the role of Papageno) and gave men what in many respects appears to be a quasi-religious experience.[18]

PETER HORWATH

Arizona State University, Tempe

NOTES

[1] Erich Schmidt, *Richardson, Rousseau, Goethe: Ein Beitrag zur Geschichte des Romans im 18. Jahrhundert* (Jena: Fromann, 1924), p. 6.

[2] *The History of Sir Charles Grandison*, 6 vols., ed. with an introd. Jocelyn Harris (London: Oxford Univ. Press, 1972), xl. The following editions of two other novels by Richardson were used: *Pamela*, introd. William M. Sale, Jr., the Norton Library (New York: Norton [1958]); *Clarissa*, 4 vols., Everyman's Library, 882 (London: Dent/New York: Dutton [n.d.]).

[3] Additional, and today forgotten authors are: Dusch, Timme, Wezel, Trütschler, and Müller.

[4] I have not been able to locate any information about how large they were, how many translations were made, and the volume in terms of sales, but in his reply to Nicolai refered to on p. 100, Friedel mentions at least three German editions by the summer of 1783.

[5] For details about Friedel's life, see esp. G. Gugitz, "Johann Friedel," *Jahrbuch der Grillparzer-Gesellschaft*, XV (1905), 186-250. Additional information is to be found in Meusel, Ersch und Gruber, *ADB*, and Goedeke.

[6] Gugitz, op. cit., 204.

[7] Quoted after Gugitz, op. cit., 212.

[8] "Ein Brief an Herrn Nikolai in Berlin. Preßburg den 15ten July 1783", in *Johann Friedels gesammelte kleine gedruckte und ungedruckte Schriften*, 1784, pp. 224-6.

[9] Contrary to Gugitz, I do not believe that Pastor Hamoniens is Lessing's opponent Pastor Goeze.

[10] Friedel seems to be subscribing to this view, although he protests against the ruler's interference in matters of the heart.

[11] Cf. also the Richardson-inspired novel *Geschichte des Fräuleins von Sternheim* by Sophie von La Roche, who, incidentally, has Spaa as the scene of her novel's action. La Roche insists on having her characters come from the upper classes.

[12] As Richardson's novels are virtually domestic conduct books, his heroines are shown as being educated, playing instruments; as writing, singing, and doing needle-work. Such details are absent from *Eleonore*.

[13] One wonders whether Mozart knew *Eleonore* and its author.

[14] Quoted after "Heroes of the Divided Mind: Eighteenth-Century English Versions of Madame de Lafayette's Duke de Nemours" by Prof. Mildred S. Greene, who kindly permitted me to make use of her unpublished paper.

[15] *Pamela* strikes a Christian note: in death everyone is equal because we are all facing the same judge. Nevertheless, Richardson did believe that "those marriages are generally happiest in which equality of birth and degree are attended to" (S. Richardson, *A Collection of the Moral and Instructive Sentiments, Maxims . . . Contained in Pamela, Clarissa, and Sir Charles Grandison* (London: Printed for S. Richardson, 1755), p. 51.

[16] Only this character is assigned an initial. Perhaps this is a device to create the illusion of reality; the crime was of such a horrible nature that the author was obliged to protect the count by keeping his family name from the public.

[17] Gugitz, op. cit., 211.

[18] I would like to thank Kathryn L. Genteman and Peter Branscombe for their help with this article.

II

CULTURAL LIFE IN
EARLY NINETEENTH-CENTURY VIENNA

Both politically and culturally, a watershed in the life of Biedermeier Vienna was clearly reached in the early 1830s, when the reverberations of the July Revolution in Paris coincided with the death, within a few years of each other, of some of the most brilliant figures in the artistic life of "Alt-Wien". A letter written by Moriz von Schwind after the death of Schubert in November 1828 expresses the feelings of their whole circle: "Schubert ist tot und mit ihm das Heiterste und Schönste, das wir hatten" (Deutsch, p. 569).[1] In 1830 two popular young actresses died: in June the Burgtheater tragedienne Sophie Müller, in December Therese Krones, star of the Theater in der Leopoldstadt. In 1832, after eighteen years as *Hoftheatersecretär*, Schreyvogel fell victim to cholera; and in 1836 Raimund committed suicide. The golden age of Viennese Biedermeier extends, then, from just after the Congress of Vienna to the mid-thirties or thereabouts; among the questions to be asked about it are: first, whether it really was a golden age, or whether Vienna was the "Kapua der Geister" that Grillparzer—perhaps the only major Viennese dramatist of the time who retained a searing capacity for self-criticism and a punishingly keen sense of form—termed it in 1843 in his poem "Abschied von Wien"; and secondly, whether the cultural institutions of the period contributed to the debilitating effect ascribed to the city in that poem, to the erosion of strict standards.

In 1828 Karl Postl (Charles Sealsfield) published his account of *Austria as it is*. Following immediately after his discussion of Grillparzer come the following comments:

> A more fettered being than an Austrian author surely never existed. A writer in Austria must not offend against any Government; nor against any minister; nor against any hierarchy, if its members be influential; nor against the aristocracy. He must not be liberal—nor philosophical—nor humorous—in short, he must be nothing at all. Under the catalogue of offences, are comprehended not only satires, and witticisms; —nay, he must not explain things at all, because they might lead to serious thoughts. . . . What would have become of Shakspeare had he been doomed to live or to write in Austria? (209 f.)

The answer to this rhetorical question is, no doubt, that he would have muddled along, like everyone else, but that he would certainly have written works very different from those he did write—which is precisely why the cultural environment repays investigation.

It hardly needs to be said that in the age of Raimund and Grillparzer Vienna was a city with a flourishing theatrical life, nor that in the age of Beethoven and Schubert it was a city of music. What Mozart wrote to his father on 4 April 1781—that Vienna was "*für mein Metier* der beste Ort von der Welt"—long held true: even the critical Sealsfield conceded that "A new opera of Rossini in the [Kärntnertor] theatre will, with these good people, produce quite as much and even more excitement than the opening of the Parliament in London" (p. 203). In 1840 Stifter recorded in his sketch "Wiener Salonszenen" in *Wien und die Wiener* that Vienna still retained its reputation of being "die Stadt der Musik, guter Musik und in erlesenen Zirkeln auch *verstandener* Musik"; and in the salon he portrays everyone present is a musician, capable of playing the piano or the violin or some other instrument. One of the figures there is Grillparzer, who used to improvise on the piano—"mit ebenso viel Talent als Geschmack" according to one account (Pichler, *Denkwürdigkeiten*, II, 114), though this must be set against a more sober report that he would play (more like the hero of *Der arme Spielmann*) "ganz nach seinem Sinne, bald zu schnell, bald zu langsam" (*Gespräche*, III, 150).

It is less well remembered that Vienna was also a centre for an outstanding generation of painters born in the years around the turn of the century. The museums and galleries of the city—the Österreichische Galerie, the Historisches Museum der Stadt Wien, the Niederösterreichisches Landesmuseum—contain a rich display of genre-paintings (by Ferdinand Georg Waldmüller, Peter Fendi, Josef Danhauser and others) and portraits (Waldmüller, Danhauser, Leopold Kupelwieser, Josef Kriehuber, Friedrich von Amerling), as well as the miniatures of Moritz Daffinger and the illustrations of Schwind. There are landscapes of the Vienna Woods and Niederösterreich (Waldmüller, Danhauser, Stifter, Josef Schwemminger, Friedrich Gauermann), and scenes of Vienna itself (Rudolf von Alt, Franz Alt, and in an older generation Franz Scheyerer, Alois von Saar, Jakob Alt). The artists who attempted paintings of Vienna could look back on the classic example of the Venetian Bellotto, nine of whose Viennese views hang in the Kunsthistorisches Museum; and indeed generations of artists were inspired by the beauty of the city and its setting, and by the intimate character of the centre.[2]

The position of the Burgtheater in the Michaelerplatz (until the opening of the present building on the *Ringstraße* in 1888) was symbolical of the central place of the theatre in Viennese life. Hüttner has recently urged caution towards the reputation of early nineteenth-century Vienna as a theatre-mad city; and certainly the growth of the population between 1800 and 1850 was not reflected in a corresponding increase in the number of theatres. That the incomers to the *Vorstädte* were not absorbed in the regular audiences of the popular theatres is, indeed, one of the reasons for the decline of the *Volkskomödie*; but it cannot be doubted that within the indigenous population enthusiastic interest in the theatre extended through all levels of society, from the artisan classes of the *Vorstädte* to the court itself. On 26 December 1807 Schreyvogel's weekly *Das Sonntagsblatt* contained a fictitious letter to the editor which purported to complain about the constant

strain of being visited during an illness and added "Nur während der Theater-
zeit habe ich immer ein wenig Erhohlung"; and thirty years later Frances
Trollope, who found the Vienna of the mid-1830s suffering from "an access
of waltzes" (I, 285), similarly found that at the height of Fasching playgoing
provided an occasional respite (II, 129). This is one field in which artists
had to reckon with a public with lively expectations. Even in the Burgtheater the tradition established by Schreyvogel was that the theatre was
not merely a literary form but above all a medium of entertainment: in
Grillparzer's words, "Um des Publikums willen ist das Theater da";[3] and
this convention contributed to the persistently mixed character of the
audience, none of the theatres being exclusively for a limited section of the
public. Hüttner argues convincingly that the audience of each of the popular
theatres was to a large extent localized; nevertheless a measure of overlap
in audiences was clearly a vital precondition for that cross-fertilization of
theatrical practitioners evidenced both in popular parody, which depended
on a knowledge in the *Vorstadttheater* audience of the repertory of the Burgtheater and the opera-house, and in a play such as *Der Traum ein Leben*,
based on the essentially popular convention of the *Besserungsstück*.

This distinctive social blend in the theatre audiences is symptomatic of
an important quality in the whole cultural ambience of the city. Making
this point, Friedrich Heer observes that at the very time when the traditional
structure of society in Western Europe was beginning to disintegrate in the
aftermath of the Industrial Revolution, what was being attempted in Vienna
was a bridging of the cultural gap long found between the "two nations"
in every major country, a meeting and a blend between the culture of the
people, uneducated and underprivileged, and the international culture of
the court and the educated classes. It is this dialogue, he argues, this blend-
ing of cultural experience—a dialogue pursued in Vienna with unique persis-
tence from the seventeenth century onwards—that produced the peculiar
character of Viennese music and was continued in the popular theatre.[4]

Yet Sealsfield could declare: "Never, perhaps, has there been exhibited
an example of so complete and refined a despotism in any civilized country
as in Austria" (p. vi). The very centrality of the theatre in the life of Vienna
meant that the censorship laws were imposed with particular severity in the
theatre. In June 1815, when Schreyvogel was adapting Kotzebue's historical
drama *Rudolph von Habsburg und König Ottokar von Böhmen* for production
in the Theater an der Wien, he wrote to Kotzebue: "Es ist unglaublich,
welche Schwierigkeiten die hiesige Zensur der Beförderung des Neuen in den
Weg setzt", and pleaded: "Möchte es Ihnen doch gefallen, bei der Wahl
Ihrer Sujets einige Rücksicht auf unsre politischen und kirchlichen Verhält-
nisse zu nehmen!"[5] If Grillparzer chose to write a drama on the same theme,
well aware though his mentor was of the censorship problem, he had only
himself to blame if its production was delayed by the censor for over a year;
and after that experience we may well credit that when casting around for

his next dramatic subject, he was concerned to choose "denjenigen Stoff . . ., der mir die wenigsten Zensurschwierigkeiten darzubieten schien" (*Selbst-biographie*, p. 180). It was shortly after this, in 1828, that Sealsfield commented: "Should an Austrian author dare to write contrary to the views of the Government, his writings would be not only mutilated, but he himself regarded as a contagious person, with whom no faithful subject should have any intercourse . . ." (p. 210); and a year after that Grillparzer wrote in his diary: "Ein östreichischer Dichter sollte höher gehalten werden als jeder andere. Wer unter solchen Umständen den Muth nicht ganz verliert, ist wahrlich eine Art Held."[6] Not every author was of heroic stuff; among those who came to terms with the censorship not by resistance but by collaboration, accepting posts as censors, were both Schreyvogel (from 1817 onwards) and Johann Ludwig Deinhardstein (from 1829 till 1848).

Though the censorship exercised under Metternich's government was principally designed to serve conservative political ends, it also protected the Establishment in other spheres, a notable example being the rejection in 1815 of a proposed production of *Nathan der Weise* in the Burgtheater when the Archbishop of Vienna objected that its moral, enshrined specifically in the allegory of the three rings, was offensive to the Christian religion. (When the play was finally produced in 1819, it was in a bowdlerized form, from which all the passages offensive to the archbishop had been expunged.)[7] The severity, and frequent arbitrariness, of the censorship had important effects on the whole field of communications and the exchange of opinion. In particular, the wide-ranging freedom of the press established by Josef II ended swiftly in the 1790s when a number of "Jacobins" were arrested and executed in the course of 1793-4. The Jacobin radicals in Vienna had included none of the important men of letters of the Josephinian period and had had no popular support; but with the Court and the police hypersensitive to radicalism and separatism (especially in Hungary), it was under a year after Franz II's succession that a decree dated 9 February 1793 proscribed all books presenting the French Revolution in a favourable light, and any favourable mention of the French Revolution in Austrian newspapers.[8] The fate of the *Österreichische Monatsschrift*, which came to an end with the number for June 1794 (edited by Schreyvogel) was typical of the plight of liberal journals. In 1801 the administration of censorship was taken over by the Ministry of Police, and in the first three decades of the nineteenth century Vienna lacked any serious organ of intellectual opinion. Indeed, there was not even a political newspaper to comment on the events of the Napoleonic period; and for satirical comment the reading public had to rely largely on the dialect comedy of the *Eipeldauerbriefe* from the pens of a succession of popular dramatists—Josef Richter (a Josephinian reformist) till 1813, then Franz X. Gewey till 1819, then Adolf Bäuerle till 1821. One of the most widely read journals commenting on the cultural life of the city, Bäuerle's *Theaterzeitung*, which was founded in 1806 and lasted through the

1850s, similarly aimed to entertain rather than to sustain a high level of informed comment. The standard even of theatre criticism was on the whole low—whether in the *Theaterzeitung*, or in the *Modenzeitung* (1816-48), or in *Der Sammler*, edited from 1809-1813 by Castelli, then by Josef von Seyfried; and precisely the level of criticism—dilettante, philistine, even corrupt—was satirized by Bauernfeld in his comedy *Der literarische Salon* of 1836.

If the free discussion of ideas was not possible in print, it was also restricted in oral form. Castelli recalls in his memoirs (II, 63) how difficult it was under the Metternich régime for groups to meet regularly without being infiltrated by police spies. In the Josephinian period, liberal men of letters had regularly gathered in the Kramersches Kaffeehaus in the Schlosser-gaßl, off the Graben, where foreign newspapers and periodicals were available; and many of the leading figures of rationalist and liberal leanings—men such as Alxinger, Blumauer and Sonnenfels—had also been Freemasons, with regular contact through membership of Masonic lodges. Membership of a Masonic lodge served not least as an expression of the humane and optimistic idealism celebrated in *Die Zauberflöte* and Blumauer's poems, and the lodges were consolidated and protected by an imperial decree; but they too fell to the anti-Jacobin reaction, being subjected to such strong pressure from the Ministry of Police under Count Johann Anton von Pergen that by the end of 1793 all meetings had come to an end. At the same time police supervision of other public meeting-places, including the coffee-houses, was so intensified that free political discussion was effectively restricted to the privacy of the home. In the Metternich period, though clubs were formed, they often flourished only briefly, and enjoyed a chequered history. The best-remembered club of the 1820s was the *Ludlamshöhle*, which grew out of an informal group of literary and artistic friends who met in conversation and discussion, and which was given its formal title after the première of Oehlenschläger's *Ludlams Höhle* in the Theater an der Wien in December 1817. Once formally organized, the club met principally in an inn in the Schlossergaßl, and its hundred or so members included a large number of prominent figures from the literary and theatrical world, including Castelli, Deinhardstein, Zedlitz and the actor Heinrich Anschütz. The concern of the club as defined to the police by Anschütz was "Zerstreuung durch Unter-haltung, Unterhaltung durch geistreichen Scherz und Erleichterung der Ver-dauung durch Lachen" (*Erinnerungen*, p. 249); but it was long under police observation: a detailed police report on its activities has survived dating from as early as 1822 (Zausmer, pp. 97 f.). In mid-April 1826, a month after Grillparzer had been admitted to full membership, it was raided under suspicion of being a centre of political activity. That the suspicion was in fact without foundation—that the club had merely the character of "eine heitere Tisch-gesellschaft" (Anschütz, p. 242)—seems typical of the political torpor of the times: up to the 1830s, as Bauernfeld recalls in his memoirs (p. 216), social gatherings in Vienna remained "harmlos und gemütlich". Yet the members of the *Ludlamshöhle* were subjected to interrogation and house-arrest, and the club was disbanded.

Inns and taverns continued to be favourite meeting-places for artists, including notoriously in the early Biedermeier period the Bohemian poet Ferdinand Sauter. The inn most noteworthy for its artistic associations was the Gasthaus zum "Stern", in the Brandstätte, where Bauernfeld's circle met regularly from the early 1830s onwards and where for two or three years, until the embittering failure of *Weh dem, der lügt!*, Grillparzer was often of the company. The memoirs of Bauernfeld, Castelli and L. A. Frankl record various later attempts to found more formal clubs: the "Concordia" of the early 1840s, whose members included Nestroy, Friedrich Kaiser, Grillparzer, Waldmüller, and the actor Ludwig Löwe, the "Soupiritum" or "Gnomen-höhle", and later in the 1850s the "Grüne Insel". Frankl records that in the 1840s a representative of the police was regularly in attendance at the "Concordia", to ensure that there was no political content in the meetings (pp. 265-7); he also suggests that the memory of the "Ludlamshöhle" affair may have influenced the decision of the Chief of the State Police, Count Sedlnitzky, not to close the "Concordia" down, in anticipation of the furore that such an action would have caused (pp. 272 f.). The one society of intellectual and political significance in the 1840s was a very different affair, the *Juridisch-politischer Leseverein*. Founded in 1841 in response to an application made by 15 prominent jurists to establish a library of law period-icals, it developed into a society of over 200 members drawn from a wide range of professions, though there was little overlap with the artistic clubs. Quickly acquiring a reputation as a centre of liberal ideas, it was regarded with grave suspicion by Sedlnitzky, who forbade the taking of several German papers in 1846 and late in 1847 instigated a productive raid on the club library.

All these essentially male societies are untypical of the increasingly im-portant role played by women in literary life from the late eighteenth century onwards, an influence whose classic expression was the salon. The salon of Charlotte von Greiner, where the Josephinian liberals in Vienna would meet, broke up in the mid-1790s; but later Frau von Greiner attended the salon of her daughter, Caroline Pichler, which was held in a house in the Alser-straße from 1800 onwards. An idealized example of the early nineteenth-century salon is given by Schreyvogel in his sketches of discussions in the house of "Frau von Norberg", where one would meet "eine Auswahl der gebildetsten Einwohner Wiens und der interessanten Fremden, welche un-sere Stadt besuchen", and where only occasionally would argument on particularly burning matters of literary and theatrical interest degenerate into "antikritische Heftigkeit".[9] Schreyvogel had been introduced to the salon of Frau von Greiner in the early 1790s, and from about 1815 renewed contact in Caroline Pichler's salon. Caroline Pichler, herself a prolific writer, did not pretend to a formidable intellectualism, but rather was adept at steering the conversation of her guests—a skill to which Castelli pays tribute when he describes her as having been "nie mürrisch, nie geschwätzig, nie unbescheiden, in einer literarischen Gesellschaft nie sich vordrängend, aber auch nie im Gespräche zurückbleibend" (*Memoiren*, II, 282). She was justly proud of the lively circle she maintained, which was one of the principal focal points of the cultural life of Alt-Wien:

> In mein Haus kommen manche sehr vorzügliche Menschen, sehr edle, hochgebildete Frauen, die deßhalb doch um keine Linie aus dem Kreise schöner Weiblichkeit vorgeschritten sind, gelehrte, würdige Männer, Künstler, Beamte, Krieger, und ich kann mit Lust und Stolz sagen, es ist zuweilen ein erlesener Zirkel, wie man ihn selten—selbst in Wien—beysammen findet, in meinem Besuchzimmer versammelt.[10]

Her salon offered recitations, theatricals and musical evenings, as well as literary conversation. For over twenty years it was held twice weekly; then from the mid-twenties she would invite rather smaller groups, until the regular gatherings effectively came to an end with her husband's death in 1837. Her guests included nearly all the leading writers of the Vormärz. The dominant figures included Hormayr, Deinhardstein, Schreyvogel, and Josef von Hammer-Purgstall; later Anschütz and Frankl. Grillparzer was introduced by Schreyvogel not long after the première of *Die Ahnfrau*, and was for a short time a regular guest; as her letter of 11 December 1819 to Therese Huber testifies, Caroline Pichler enjoyed encouraging young artists —"junge hoffnungsvolle Leute"—and was confident "daß ich schon manches Gute auf diese Art gestiftet".

Though Frances Trollope met Caroline Pichler in 1837, the salons to which she found entrée were in the main those of high society. Here she found that literary matters were not the stuff of general discussion. She was introduced to "one or two authors"; but as for "the general tone of conversation in good society", she had to admit after two and a half months in Vienna that she had "never yet heard anything approaching to general conversation take a literary turn, excepting indeed at the French ambassador's" (II, 40). Of course the nobility in the capital of the polyglot Habsburg Empire were cultured and had international horizons; even Sealsfield admitted "There will scarcely be an Austrian nobleman who does not read and write the English, French and Italian languages perfectly well" (p. 225). Mrs Trollope too observed that the Viennese were widely read, in several languages; she found in particular "that the majority of the educated classes of both sexes read English" and reported: "I do not believe there is any country, where English is not the spoken language, in which Shakespeare is so thoroughly understood and appreciated as here" (II, 38)—a propitious audience, then, for Grillparzer's histories. But Mrs Trollope's circles were ill-informed about the domestic literary scene. "It seems to be acknowledged on all hands that Austrian poets do not abound", she noted (II, 183—this in 1837!) and identified as the "poet par excellence of Austria" Zedlitz, "the admired translator of Childe Harold . . ." (II, 185). Zedlitz had recently dedicated this translation to Metternich, and Mrs Trollope's acceptance of the praise lavished on him in high society is one of many examples of her political gullibility; but the trouble lay also, perhaps, in a circumstance that Mme de Staël had remarked on after her visit of 1806-7, when she wrote in *De l'Allemagne* that one of the chief disadvantages of Viennese society was that the aristocracy and the men of letters did not mix and commented: "Il résulte de cette séparation de classes que les gens de lettres manquent de grâce, et que les gens du monde acquièrent rarement l'instruction."[11]

Less philistine circles than those met by Mrs Trollope were to be found in several houses noted for their musical evenings, among them notably in the 1820s the home of Schubert's friend Josef von Spaun.[12] It was at a musical evening elsewhere that Grillparzer is supposed to have met Katharina Fröhlich: at the Palais Caprara-Geymüller in the Wallnerstraße, not far from the Hofburg. This building, which now houses the British Consulate, belonged in the early nineteenth century to the banker Johann Heinrich Geymüller; the salon in Empire style, rich in gilt, ormolu and marble, has been preserved and reconstructed in the Historisches Museum. Equally famous were the salons in the houses of other bankers, all belonging to cultured Jewish families, where aristocrats and diplomats were leavened with a select few men of learning: the salons of Fanny von Arnstein (famous for the extravagance of the entertainmemts around the time of the Congress of Vienna), of her younger sister Cäcilie von Eskeles, and of her daughter Henriette von Pereira. The latter's weekly *Künstlersoirées* were in level the closest equivalent to the salon of Caroline Pichler, who would herself sometimes attend and warmly admired Henriette von Pereira's salon as one "wo ein ungezwungener Ton herrschte, viele Jugend sich versammelte, und Musik, Tanz, Vorlesen eine lebhafte Abwechslung der Unterhaltung boten" (*Denkwürdigkeiten*, II, 124). Henriette von Pereira was compared by Castelli to Ottilie von Goethe as a guaranteed provider of "geistreiche und gesellige Unterhaltung" (*Memoiren*, II, 145); hers is indeed the salon commemorated in Stifter's sketch "Wiener Salonszenen", which describes an attractive scene, with Grillparzer and Hammer among the identifiable guests, with an informal atmosphere based on conversation and with no formal prepared performances.

In the 1830s and 1840s, so Bauernfeld's memoirs record (p. 216), Hammer was himself one of the principal hosts of the literary world. Early in 1837 Mrs Trollope spent an evening at the house of "*the* Asiatic Hammer", where Hammer's collection of oriental manuscripts and books was on display, and she adjudged the party "more fairly coming under the description of a conversazione than most meetings intended to be such" (II, 111). Hammer's circle, however, was predominantly male, and this is symptomatic of the decline of the true salon. Though the tradition lived on into the last quarter of the nineteenth century, most notably in the hospitality of Josefine von Wertheimstein, the importance of the salon as an institution declined as that of the coffee-house increased. Even in Caroline Pichler's time the more hot-headed of the younger writers, like Bauernfeld and Lenau, did not keep up their attendance at her salon (*Denkwürdigkeiten*, II, 311), clearly preferring the less formal and more relaxed atmosphere of the coffee-house. Frankl (p. 105) records that in the near-retirement of her last years Caroline Pichler regretted this trend, lamenting "daß die jüngeren Dichter es vorzogen, im 'silbernen Kaffeehause' in der Plankengasse der inneren Stadt im Tabakqualme 'wie die Götter in Wolken', statt in einem Salon neben anmutigen, geistigen Frauen zu sitzen".

The coffee-house is, at its best, "eine Art demokratischer, jedem für eine billige Schale Kaffee zugänglicher Klub, wo jeder Gast für diesen kleinen Obolus stundenlang sitzen, diskutieren, schreiben . . . und vor allem eine unbegrenzte Zahl von Zeitungen und Zeitschriften konsumieren kann" (Stefan Zweig).[13] A series of these institutions played an important role in the artistic life of the city. The first literary coffee-house in Vienna was the Kramersches Kaffeehaus, which was much visited for its array of journals from the 1760s onwards; after the anti-Jacobin period, when even argument about events in France was forbidden and coffee-house keepers were required to report offenders to the police,[14] Ignaz Neuner's "Silbernes Kaffeehaus", on the corner of the Plankengasse and Spiegelgasse, took over from about 1808 as a regular meeting-place of the intelligentsia. From about 1825 into the early 1840s it was also a centre of liberal ideas. Regular guests included Zedlitz, Lenau, Schwind, Auersperg, Feuchtersleben, Grillparzer and Bauernfeld. The journalists of the *Theaterzeitung* favoured another coffee-house in the *innere Stadt*, the Café Adami, while Bauernfeld seems to have been a *Stammgast* at several, including in the 1820s (with Schwind, Feuchtersleben, Schubert and their circle) the Bognersches Kaffeehaus, on the corner of the Singerstraße and the Blutgasse, and from about 1840 (with a predominantly theatrical circle including Deinhardstein, Castelli, Bäuerle and Löwe) Katzmayer's coffee-house near the Kärntnertor-Theater. By this time liberal ideas were much more openly discussed, and in December 1841 Bauernfeld noted in his diary: "Die politische Idee wird immer lebhafter in mir und läßt mir keine Ruhe. . . In jeder Gesellschaft bin ich der Vorschimpfer" (*JbGrGes* V, 95). Katzmayer's coffee-house was in fact a centre for men of letters in 1848; and by then Heinrich Griensteidl had opened in the Herrengasse what was to be the most famous of all the literary coffee-houses.

When Schubert returned to Vienna in October 1825 after a summer holiday, Bauernfeld noted in his diary: "Schubert ist zurück. Gast- und Kaffeehaus-Leben mit den Freunden, häufig bis zwei, drei Uhr des Morgens" (*JbGrGes* V, 21). Although it was rare for Schubert to stay out so late, the picture is familiar enough in his circle. The legendary self-indulgence of Viennese life survived unabated all the bureaucracy, censorship and police spying of the Metternich era; there is a certain aptness in the fact that from 1804 to 1823 the city was presided over by a mayor called Stefan von Wohlleben. What Bauernfeld, a prominent liberal, commented on amid the gaiety was the general indifference to public affairs: "Das dicke Wien mit seinem Strauß-, Lanner- und Sperl-Dusel und dem Scholz- und Nestroy-Kultus bekümmerte sich auch blutwenig um öffentliche Dinge" (*Aus Alt- und Neu-Wien*, p. 97); and Laube, who celebrated "Sperl in Floribus" in his *Reisenovellen*, found the paucity of the "geistige Welt" in Vienna out of keeping with the size of the city (*Grillparzers Gespräche*, III, 65). In an age of financial instability, with inflation unrelenting and speculation and social injustice rife, hedonistic escapism was the easy alternative to revolution; Mrs Trollope was only one of many observers who perceived that "Far from checking this universal spirit of gaiety, the wise government of Austria fosters it, as one of the surest means of keeping the minds of the people from . . . gloomy discontent" (II, 134 f.).

Any common national character in "the minds of the people" is probably no more than myth; but myths are powerful, and the Austrians certainly see themselves as possessing an earthy common sense, "gesunder Menschenverstand". Grillparzer was one who saw this as a distinctively Austrian characteristic (e.g. "Abschied von Wien"). The Austrian sees himself as leaning to understatement, and his earthy dialect lends itself to contrasts with over-seriousness and to the deflation of sentimentality. Bauernfeld makes this point in a series of comic examples in a poem entitled "Wiener Dialekt";[15] and it is one of the basic ingredients of the long tradition of Viennese parody.

Hüttner has argued that most of the parodies performed in the popular theatres were not so much critical parodies as trivializations of serious originals, popularizations for the less educated *Vorstadt* public. This, however, fails to hold good of several important examples: of Meisl's *Die Frau Ahndel*, which was admittedly not a box-office success; of Nestroy's parodies, even in the 1830s (*Robert der Teuxel, Die verhängnisvolle Faschingsnacht*: Hüttner sees Nestroy as untypical of the tradition);[16] and of F. X. Told's parody of *Sappho*, which was first performed on 24 October 1818 in the Theater in der Josefstadt, was praised in the *Wiener Zeitschrift* on 29 October as one of the best parodies staged in that theatre and lived on in the repertory for nearly fifteen years. Though the text is lost, the substance of this work can be pieced together from the review in the *Wiener Zeitschrift* and that two days later in the *Theaterzeitung*.[17] What is striking is the sureness with which it evidently picked out for parody the weak points in Grillparzer's tragedy. Thus in Act III of the parody—reversing the roles of the original, where it is Sappho who comes upon the sleeping Phaon—Phaunzel discovers that his betrothed has false teeth, artificial hair and a glass eye—a comic exaggeration of the ageing quality of the original Sappho (and, perhaps, of the tragedienne Sophie Schröder). The sharpest critical shafts are directed at the ending. When Told's Seppherl finally forgives the young lovers, she remembers the Sappho of the tragedy and goes off to die a sacrificial death herself by enlisting as a dragoon, to die for her fatherland—the unclear logic of this, after the reconciliation, clearly serving to suggest the obscure motivation of the original. In Told's Second Act, moreover, a troupe of strolling players perform Grillparzer's *Sappho*, and after the heroine has performed her leap from the Leucadian rock she is applauded, and performs the leap again as an encore—a device to suggest that the ending of the original is no more than a stagy trick.

The scepticism of the Viennese towards what might seem like pretentiousness of sentiment or language is undying. It is to be found ironically affirmed in the dialect poem "Leitspruch" introducing Weinheber's collection *Wien wörtlich* of 1935. The danger inherent in this scepticism is that, even in a city with the rich artistic life of early nineteenth-century Vienna, it could degenerate into an automatic philistinism. The masterpieces of Viennese parody are acute in their perception of the false and overblown; but was there an over-eagerness to parody? Could the serious artist count on being appreciated seriously? — On 27 July 1831 the periodical *Der Gesellschafter* announced that Grillparzer had completed a new play, summarized the form it was to take, and added: "Das Stück wird sich gut parodieren lassen" (*Gespräche*, III, 15). This automatic reaction smacks of a certain complacency; and complacency is a vice that many critical observers, from Nicolai in the 1780s onwards, have been quick to sense in the Viennese, even in their theatrical life. One particularly distinctive kind was noticed by Brentano in the Napoleonic period, in relation to the starry-eyed fascination of the Viennese public with their actors: " 'Mein Gott! Wie können sich die Wiener Hoffnung machen, Napoleon zu schlagen, da sie so viel Wohlgefallen an . . . (ich weiß nicht mehr, welchen mittelmäßigen Schauspieler er hier nannte) finden!' " (Pichler, *Denkwürdigkeiten*, I, 424). A century later Karl Kraus was to portray the public of the First World War period still absorbed with actors and operetta stars while the apocalyptic "last days of mankind" remained uncomprehended; in the mid-nineteenth century Bauernfeld, reviewing the prospects of the popular theatres, concluded gloomily: "Die Stücke . . . sind nichts—die Persönlichkeit der Schauspieler ist Alles."[18] Indeed, in the popular theatres as well as the Burgtheater there were some extraordinary examples of the public's lack of discrimination: for instance, the success of Told's *Der Zauberschleier*, which received a hundred performances *en suite*, two hundred within a year, and over four hundred in all, by contrast with the relative failure of *Des Meeres und der Liebe Wellen* and *Liebesgeschichten und Heiratssachen*. That the same public who could be so extraordinarily receptive of art could also be indifferent to it is a paradoxical phenomenon not restricted to the theatre, and indeed notoriously illustrated in the long neglect of Mozart's burial-place.

The lack of a final commitment to art—taking it for granted because it was all around, and therefore in the last analysis not taking it seriously enough—readily infected the practitioners, the writers and dramatists. And here the cultural life of the capital surely has a responsibility to bear: the standard of criticism in the press; the curiously middle-brow and apolitical quality even of Caroline Pichler's salon; the restrictions on information and comment. Even the shackles of censorship—as satirists as far apart as Schreyvogel and Nestroy pointed out—could be used as a shield, unproductiveness being defended with the excuse "Ich wollte wohl schreiben, wenn ich nur dürfte!" (*Das Sonntagsblatt*, 31 May 1807) or "Ach Gott! Es is schrecklich, sie verbieten einem ja alles" (*Freiheit in Krähwinkel*, I, 7). To writers unharried by reviewers of stature, encouraged by an easy-going public and certainly restricted in their active political enthusiasms by the censors, coffee-houses and taverns provided an easy form of escapism, a buffer against the creative conscience; and even the awareness of indolence could merge into the bittersweet mood of self-indulgent enjoyment summarized in a short poem with which Bauernfeld continues the diary-note recording Schubert's return and its late-night celebration:

> Wirthshaus, wir schämen uns,
> Hat uns ergötzt;
> Faulheit, wir grämen uns,
> Hat uns geletzt.

W. E. YATES

Exeter

Bibliographical Note

Information about the informal side of the cultural life in Vienna in the Biedermeier period may be gathered from diverse sources. Among the most important of the primary sources are the memoirs of prominent members of the artistic circles: Heinrich Anschütz, *Erinnerungen aus dessen Leben und Wirken*, ed. Roderich Anschütz (Leipzig, n.d. [1900]); Eduard von Bauernfeld, *Aus Alt- und Neu-Wien* (1873), in Bauernfeld, *Ausgewählte Werke*, ed. E. Horner (4 vols., Leipzig, n.d.), Vol. IV; Ignaz Franz Castelli, *Memoiren meines Lebens. Gefundenes und Empfundenes, Erlebtes und Erstrebtes* (ed. J. Bindtner, 2 vols., Munich, 1914); L. A. Frankl, *Erinnerungen*, ed. Stefan Hock (Prague, 1910); Friedrich Kaiser, *Unter fünfzehn Theater-Direktoren. Bunte Bilder aus der Wiener Bühnenwelt* (Vienna, 1870); Caroline Pichler, *Denkwürdigkeiten aus meinem Leben* (ed. E. K. Blümml, 2 vols., Munich, 1914); and Grillparzer's autobiography (1853), which is quoted from the useful annotated edition by L. Böck and W. Englmann (*Grillparzers Selbstbiographie und Bildnisse*, Vienna, 1923).

These memoirs are complemented by the diaries of Bauernfeld, extracts of which up to 1848 edited by Carl Glossy are printed in the *Jahrbuch der Grillparzer-Gesellschaft* (abbreviated *JbGrGes*) V (1895), 1-217; by the material assembled by O. E. Deutsch in *Schubert. Die Dokumente seines Lebens* (Kassel, 1964) and by A. Sauer in *Grillparzers Gespräche und die Charakteristiken seiner Persönlichkeit durch die Zeitgenossen*, 7 vols. (Vols. 1-6, Vienna, 1904-16; Vol. 7 = *JbGrGes* [Neue Folge] I [1941]); by the accounts of travellers, of which Laube's *Reisenovellen* (1833) and Frances Trollope's *Vienna and the Austrians* (2 vols., Paris, 1838) are among the most entertaining; by Sealsfield's venomous *Austria as it is* (London, 1828), Caroline Pichler's *Zeitbilder* (ed. R. Latzke, Vienna, 1924), and the sketch "Wiener Salonszenen" contributed by Stifter to *Wien und die Wiener* (1841-4).

Secondary accounts of various institutions and groups include: Gertrud Prohaska, *Der literarische Salon der Karoline Pichler* (dissertation, Vienna, 1946); Otto Zausmer, "Der Ludlamshöhle Glück und Ende", *JbGrGes* XXXIII (1935), 86-112; Reinhold

Backmann, "Vor Grillparzers letztem Verzicht", *JbGrGes* (Neue Folge) IV (1944), 93-147 (on the "Stern" circle); Gustav Gugitz, *Das Wiener Kaffeehaus. Ein Stück Kultur-und Lokalgeschichte* (Vienna, 1940); Friedrich Engel-Janosi, "Der Wiener juridisch-politische Leseverein. Seine Geschichte bis zur Märzrevolution", *Mitteilungen des Vereines für Geschichte der Stadt Wien*, IV (1923), 58-66.

Studies of individual figures that treat aspects of the cultural life of the city include: Hilde Spiel, *Fanny von Arnstein oder Die Emanzipation. Ein Frauenleben an der Jahrhundertwende 1758-1818* (Frankfurt, 1962); Hermine Cloeter, "Wo Grillparzer wohnte . . . Ein Lebensbild des Dichters", *JbGrGes* (Neue Folge) IV, 25-92; Leo Grünstein, *Moritz Michael Daffinger und sein Kreis* (Vienna, Leipzig, 1923); Karl Kobald, *Beethoven. Seine Beziehungen zu Wiens Kunst und Kultur, Gesellschaft und Landschaft* (new edition, Vienna, 1953) and *Franz Schubert und seine Zeit* (Zürich, Leipzig, Vienna, 1928); and Emil Horner, *Bauernfeld* (Leipzig, Berlin, Vienna, 1900).

Other relevant aspects of the historical background are treated by Ernst Wangermann, *From Joseph II to the Jacobin Trials* (2nd ed., London, 1969); Paul P. Bernard, *Jesuits and Jacobins. Enlightenment and Enlightened Despotism in Austria* (Urbana, Chicago, London, 1971); Ludwig Bato, *Die Juden im alten Wien* (Vienna, 1928); Josef Leitner, "Die Anfänge der Wiener Theaterkritik und der Kritiker Wilhelm Hebenstreit", *JbGrGes* XXXI, 115-37; Rudolf Hölzer, "Zeitungswesen im Vormärz" in *Deutsch-österreichische Literaturgeschichte*, ed. J. W. Nagl, J. Zeidler, E. Castle, II (1914), 852-93; Julius Marx, *Die österreichische Zensur im Vormärz* (Vienna, 1959); Johann Hüttner, "Literarische Parodie und Wiener Vorstadtpublikum vor Nestroy", *Maske und Kothurn* XVIII (1972), 99-139, and "Das Burgtheaterpublikum in der ersten Hälfte des 19. Jahrhunderts" in *Das Burgtheater und sein Publikum*, Vol. I, ed. Margret Dietrich (Vienna, 1976), 123-84 (the latter essay appeared after the present article was completed). On the social and cultural background R. Kralik and H. Schlitter, *Wien. Geschichte der Kaiserstadt und ihrer Kultur* (Vienna, 1912) and Friedrich Reischl, *Wien zur Biedermeierzeit. Volksleben in Wiens Vorstädten nach zeitgenössischen Schilderungen* (Vienna, 1921) are informative; a general account of the political history of the period is given by C. A. Macartney, *The Habsburg Empire 1790-1918* (London, 1968); and a useful select historical bibliography is given in Erich Zöllner, *Geschichte Österreichs. Von den Anfängen bis zur Gegenwart* (4th edn., Vienna, 1970).

NOTES

[1] References given in the text are to the works and editions listed in the "Bibliographical Note".

[2] Hüttner is mistaken in claiming that at the beginning of the nineteenth century Vienna was the third-largest city in the world (*Maske und Kothurn* XVIII, 101). It has indeed never been even the third-largest in Europe, and in 1800 was smaller than London, Constantinople, Paris, Naples, Moscow and Lisbon. See Tertius Chandler and Gerald Fox, *3000 Years of Urban Growth*, New York, London, 1974, pp. 322-9. Whereas Paris had a population of 600,000 at the time of the French Revolution, Vienna was still only half that size as late as the 1830s. The impression of vastness made at that time by Paris on a Viennese visitor is recorded in Grillparzer, *Sämtliche Werke*, ed. August Sauer and R. Backmann, Vienna, 1909-48, II, 10, 9. In mid-century Vienna underwent the same process of expansion as Paris did in a period of industrialization and large-scale urban development; and this too is faithfully recorded in the landscapes of the time. Views of Vienna either from Nußdorf, painted by Josef Fischer in 1822 and by Matthias Rudolf Toma in 1834, or from Grinzing, painted by Carl Agricola in 1824, show the villages as rural, with an appreciable gap of open country between them and the city. (All these paintings are in the Österreichische Galerie.) But by 1872 even a romantically conceived view of Vienna from the Wildgrube, by Schwemminger (Historisches Museum), cannot conceal that the devouring sprawl of the modern city was well under way; and the same development is illustrated in two other paintings in the same museum, one by Josef Lange showing the city at the time of the Great Exhibition, the other by Albert Zimmermann, showing the view from Ober St. Veit in about 1880.

[3] Grillparzer, *Sämtl. Wke.*, I, 14, 121. See (on Schreyvogel and the Burgtheater) W. E. Yates, "Josef Schreyvogel, critic and mentor", *Publications of the English Goethe Society* (New Series) XLIV (1974), especially pp. 99-103, and (on the popular theatres)

"Elizabethan Comedy and the Alt-Wiener Volkstheater", *Forum for Modern Language Studies* III (1967), 27-35. The distinctively visual and theatrical qualities in Austrian drama have always complicated the reception of Grillparzer's plays outside Austria, as he saw even in his own time, e.g. *Sämtl. Wke.*, I, 12/i, 270 (epigram "An die Norddeutschen").

[4] Friedrich Heer, "Josef Weinheber aus Wien", *Frankfurter Hefte* VIII (1953), especially pp. 590 f. and 600.

[5] August Sauer, *Gesammelte Reden und Aufsätze zur Geschichte der Literatur in Österreich und Deutschland*, Vienna, Leipzig, 1903, 91 f. Kotzebue's drama was performed 14 August 1815.

[6] Grillparzer, *Sämtl. Wke.*, II, 8, 332.

[7] See Karl Glossy, "Zur Geschichte der Theater Wiens I (1801 bis 1820)", *JbGrGes* XXV (1915), 188 f., 252 f.

[8] See Alfred Körner, *Die Wiener Jakobiner*, Stuttgart, 1972, p. 11.

[9] *Gesammelte Schriften von Thomas und Karl August West*, Braunschweig, 1829, II/i, pp. 85 and 137.

[10] Briefe von Caroline Pichler an Therese Huber, *JbGrGes* III, 291 f. (letter of 11 December 1819).

[11] Mme de Staël, *De l'Allemagne*, ed. La Contesse Jean de Pange avec le concours de Simone Balayé, 5 vols., Paris, 1958-60, I, 130 f.

[12] Two well-known pictures by Schwind, executed from memory in about 1868, depict a musical evening at the Spauns', with Schubert at the piano and the baritone Vogl beside him—the one an uncompleted oil, the other a drawing in which many famous figures of the period can be recognized, gathered round listening, among them Bauernfeld, Castelli, Grillparzer, Feuchtersleben, Kupelwieser and Schwind himself. Both are reproduced in Karl Kobald, *Franz Schubert und seine Zeit* (1928), facing pp. 472 and 481.

[13] Zweig, *Die Welt von Gestern. Erinnerungen eines Europäers*, London, Stockholm, 1941, p. 47.

[14] Cf. Karl Blümml and Gustav Gugitz, *Altwienerisches. Bilder und Gestalten*, Vienna, Prague, Leipzig, 1920, pp. 330 f.

[15] Bauernfeld, *Ausgewählte Werke*, ed. Emil Horner, 4 vols., Leipzig, n.d., I, 80 f.

[16] See O. Paul Straubinger, "Grillparzer in der Parodie des Alt-Wiener Volkstheaters", *JbGrGes* (3. Folge) III (1960), 115-26; Margret Dietrich, "Die Frau Ahndel", *Grillparzer-Forum Forchtenstein* (1970), 62-76; W. E. Yates, *Nestroy. Satire and Parody in Viennese Popular Comedy*, Cambridge, 1972, pp. 35-42 and 99-106.

[17] The review in the *Wiener Zeitschrift* is reprinted in Margret Dietrich, *Jupiter in Wien oder Götter und Helden der Antike im Altwiener Volkstheater*, Graz, Vienna, Cologne, 1967, pp. 46 f. A summary of the plot is given by Straubinger, op. cit., p. 122 f.

[18] "Die Wiener Volksbühne", *Österr. Blätter für Literatur und Kunst* (Beilage zur *Wiener Ztg.*), 25 April 1853, p. 101. So too Gotthard Böhm writes of conditions "in der Theaterstadt Wien, in der es immer um die Schauspieler ging und nur ganz selten um Literatur, wenn es sich um Theater handelte" (*Die Presse* 21-22 September 1974, p. 7).

III

GRILLPARZER AND THE REALIST TRADITION

General critical agreement seems at last to exist about the nature and
extent of Grillparzer's debt to the various literary and theatrical traditions
to which he was heir. The struggle to refute the old charge that he is a mere
epigone of Classicism[1] has been won, and the tendency of early scholars
such as Sauer, Reich or Strich[2] to overestimate the importance of his links
with Romanticism has been corrected, chiefly by the work of Enzinger,
Alker and Baumann,[3] who have shown conclusively that much of what had
previously been interpreted as evidence of Romantic influence is in fact
more accurately ascribed to the influence of Grillparzer's Austrian background. It is now recognized that he is primarily indebted to Weimar
Classicism, the Austrian Baroque, and the theatre of Shakespeare and Lope
de Vega, and that he successfully synthesizes the disparate elements which
he derives from each of these sources in such a way as to transcend the
influence of all of them and achieve an unmistakable individuality of his
own. But what has not yet been clearly established is the precise nature
of his relationship to contemporary and subsequent movements or periods
in German literature. Thus, some commentators see him as a transitional
figure hovering—often uncertainly and unhappily, in a kind of void with
no clear centre of gravity—between Idealism (or Classicism) and Realism;[4]
others—among recent critics most notably Ulrich Fülleborn[5]—see him, more
positively, as an early Realist; some seek refuge in the vexatious unclarities
of the term *Biedermeier*, which others reject as quite inappropriate;[6] and a
few even see him as a forerunner of German Naturalism[7] or, more vaguely,
of "die Moderne",[8] which usually turns out to mean Austrian literature of
the turn of the century. Small wonder then that an increasing number of
critics coyly avoid the problem altogether and make no serious attempt to
define his relationship to any post-Goethean movements at all.

The confusion which surrounds the problem arises partly, no doubt, from
the lack of general agreement about what the term *Biedermeier* means, and
from a sometimes too lax use of the term Naturalism which, as we shall see,
is seriously misleading when applied to Grillparzer. But further confusion
has certainly been caused by the fact that the great majority of scholars
have based their assessment of his historical position almost exclusively on
an analysis of his many-sided creative *œuvre* and have almost completely
ignored his theoretical and critical ideas. This is unfortunate, because
although it would obviously be foolish to give disproportionate weight to
a side of his work which must ultimately remain of secondary importance,
the fact is that an examination of the relevant parts of his undeservedly
neglected aesthetic and dramatic theory can be of considerable help in placing
him in his correct historical context. And the conclusion to which a review
of this material points is that Fülleborn's identification of him as an early

Realist (Frührealist)—Realism being interpreted in a wide sense to embrace
most post-classical and post-romantic literature of the nineteenth century—
has much to recommend it,[9] for the evidence of his theory, together with the
new realistic features of his plays, clearly sets him apart from his Classical
and Baroque roots, and yet his affinities with Realism remain so circum-
scribed that any attempt to associate him with the "consistent realism" of
the Naturalists or even what Fülleborn calls the *Hochrealismus* of the middle
and later part of the century must be regarded with the greatest scepticism.

The new realism of his dramatic style first becomes fully apparent in
König Ottokars Glück und Ende, the work with which he opens the mature
period of his creative career in 1823. What chiefly distinguishes this play
and most of the other major products of his maturity from the work of
Goethe and Schiller, from whom he takes over the outer form of the Classical
verse-drama, is the psychological realism of his character-portrayal and—
though this is perhaps less striking and was certainly slower to gain critical
recognition—the new realism infused into a dramatic language which is at
bottom still that of the Classical age. To the careful observer, however, a
progressive movement towards the realism of his mature period is apparent
from the very beginning of his career. Not surprisingly, the first of his plays
to be performed, *Die Ahnfrau*, written in 1816, is particularly powerfully
influenced by the popular theatrical tradition of his native city, the Baroque
Volkstheater of Vienna, to which Grillparzer himself fully acknowledged his
lifelong indebtedness.[10] But although the influence of the *Volkstheater* is
readily apparent in every one of his plays, Grillparzer is far from being
simply another suburban dramatist in the manner of, for example, Hensler,
Meisl, Gleich or Bäuerle, for he transcends the popular tradition, transform-
ing those elements of his style which are derived from it in such a way that
they appear in his works in a more refined and aesthetically superior guise.[11]
And the general effect of this transformation is to produce in his plays an
altogether less extravagant and sensational—and for that very reason more
realistic—type of drama than his predecessors in the suburban theatres had
ever done. *Die Ahnfrau* itself is of course a play still very much in the idiom
of the *Volkstheater*,[12] but after 1816 we may trace a clear development in his
work away from the style of the *Volksstück* through *Sappho* and *Das goldene
Vließ* towards the realistic style which at last emerges in *König Ottokars
Glück und Ende*.

Even in *Die Ahnfrau* however, derivative work though it be, we can
already see Grillparzer beginning to feel his way towards a more realistic
style, for not only have the crasser effects of the conventional *Volksstück*
here been toned down very considerably,[13] but much of the undeniable
power of the play springs from the, albeit still rudimentary, psychological
realism discernible in some of the speeches of Bertha and Jaromir. This
still hesitant realism in the treatment of character is then carried perceptibly
further in *Sappho*, being particularly prominent in the portrayal of the

heroine in Acts III and IV of the play where the sub-classical bombast which mars some of the early scenes falls away and Sappho emerges as a psychologically credible woman consumed by sexual jealousy. In the case of *Das goldene Vließ* we have Grillparzer's own testimony to the effect that what interested him more than anything else in the story was the psychology of Medea and the problem of constructing a convincing motivation for her infanticide.[14] Not surprisingly, therefore, we find that his psychological realism is now more in evidence than ever before, so that the trilogy confronts us with some very modern, psychologically very subtly differentiated characters. Yet *Das goldene Vließ* still cannot be described without qualification as a realistic work, because the extensive use of magical elements in it—due undoubtedly to the influence of the *Volkstheater*—and the remote setting of the work in mythical antiquity are fundamentally in conflict with the relatively realistic treatment of psychology. In *König Ottokars Glück und Ende*, however, there was no possibility of any such conflict arising, for here Grillparzer's growing enthusiasm for realism in characterization and language —now set fully ablaze by the influence of Shakespeare, which first becomes fully apparent in this play—was entirely in harmony with the comparative realism of subject-matter, setting and style which the historical drama by nature requires. It is therefore in *Ottokar* that we find the first unmistakable example of the realistic style which characterizes, in greater or lesser degree, most of the plays of his maturity and old age and which justifies his claim to be regarded as an early representative of the great Realist tradition of the nineteenth century.

The growing realism of his style was not, however, by any means the result of an unconscious or fortuitous development or even solely a matter of a growing artistic maturity on Grillparzer's part, but had a firm basis in his aesthetic and dramatic theory which was taking clear shape during these early years and which more and more directed him away from the theatrical extravagances of the *Volksstück* towards an increasingly restrained, and therefore increasingly realistic, type of writing. We have noted that even in *Die Ahnfrau* the more extreme features of the popular style had already been eliminated or significantly refined; nevertheless, Grillparzer was in no doubt that the enormous success of the play was due mainly to its sensational theatrical qualities—and about this he was not at all happy. A genuinely good poet, he felt, should be able to produce a theatrically successful play without resorting to such means; and it was for this reason, he tells us, that he set out to write in *Sappho* a very different sort of play which would be entirely free of violent effects.[15] It is therefore quite clear that even as early as 1817 his inherently refined and sensitive taste, confirmed and strengthened no doubt by his admiration for the German classics, was already rejecting as aesthetically inferior the sensational element in the *Volksstück*.[16] And there is ample evidence to show that his dislike for excessively strong theatrical effects remained with him all his life. In diary-notes made between

1828 and 1831 he censures what he regards as the inordinately violent theatrical effect of the third and fourth acts of *Ein Treuer Diener seines Herrn*[17] and the excessively theatrical conclusion of *Des Meeres und der Liebe Wellen;*[18] and in 1853, in the *Selbstbiographie*, he reaffirms his conviction that "das Bunte und Grelle eben nicht Zeichen eines guten Geschmacks [sind]".[19] Of course, he recognizes fully that the dramatist must always strive to make his play theatrically effective,[20] but there is all the difference in the world between the legitimate effect sought by any good dramatist and mere "Effektmacherei".[21] Ideally what the poet needs to do is to steer a middle course between, on the one hand, a style which lacks theatrical life and, on the other hand, a crude theatricality lacking in artistic discipline and real poetic merit. This is what he meant when he wrote: "Ich fühle mich . . . gerade jenes Mittelding zwischen Goethe und Kotzebue, wie ihn das Drama braucht."[22] And, as we may see from the example of his own plays, this middle course results in practice in a style not only dramatically superior to, but also more realistic than, that of Goethe, Kotzebue or the dramatists of the *Volkstheater*.

In addition to the conviction that the crude sensationalism of the *Volkstheater* was offensive to good taste, there was a second aspect of Grillparzer's rapidly developing theory which further strengthened his growing impulse towards a more realistic style. This was his belief, first stated in 1820 in the essay *Über das Wesen des Drama*, that the dramatic illusion, which for him is still a self-evident necessity, can be created and sustained only by strict observance of the laws of cause and effect (strenge Kausalität).[23] The heavy emphasis which he thus places on the importance of probability in the drama was something alien to the Baroque tradition of the *Volkstheater*. Here the concept of the dramatic illusion was much less important than in the tradition of literary German drama which had for so long stood under the influence of the thought and style of the French Classical dramatists and their successors and learned to share their concern for *vraisemblance*. The poets of the popular theatre had therefore rarely hesitated to depart from the laws of probability in their pursuit of the spectacular theatrical effects which for them were of the first importance in the drama. For Grillparzer, however, the creation of spectacular stage-effects regardless of the cost in terms of probability was not the paramount objective, and it was inevitable that the different intention with which he worked should result in a different, and more realistic, style of writing. This difference is already apparent even in *Die Ahnfrau*, for he makes a considerable effort—far greater than would have been made by any of the dramatists of the popular tradition—to render the supernatural element in the play plausible.[24] And in most of the rest of his plays (*Der Traum ein Leben* is the one obvious exception), a concern for probability, which is of course of the essence of his psychological realism, remains one of the most marked characteristics of his style.

While, however, it is true that Grillparzer displays definite affinities with the broad Realism of nineteenth-century literature, the point must be firmly made that his realism remains highly selective and is not to be compared with the more advanced realism of the Young Germans, Büchner, Grabbe or Hebbel, or—least of all—with the "konsequenter Realismus" of the thorough-going Naturalists of the later years of the century. Particularly mischievous is the assertion, which is now fortunately less commonly heard than it used to be but which critic after critic still feels it necessary to deny, that he is a precursor of Naturalism and has a substantial connection with that movement. Those critics who have argued for the existence of such a link have based their claims mainly on what they consider to be a Naturalistic technique of character-portrayal in some of the later dramas.[25] But—and I stress this point—all the evidence of his theory makes it perfectly clear that he emphatically rejected those trends in contemporary literature which culminated in the programme of the Naturalists and that, if he had lived long enough to see the movement, he would have abhorred everything about it.

The fact is that Grillparzer's whole conception of the relationship between art and nature is fundamentally different from that of the Naturalists, either as we find it embodied in their creative works or as it is stated, admittedly in an extreme form, in the celebrated theoretical equation of Arno Holz: "Kunst $=$ Natur $-$ X" (where "X" represents the inevitable obstacle to complete fidelity of reproduction posed by the artist's subjectivity and the limitations of the technical means at his disposal).[26] The central idea in Grillparzer's aesthetic and poetic theory is that of beauty (Schönheit) or the beautiful (das Schöne)—he uses the words interchangeably. Beauty is for him, strictly speaking, not a property which is permanently resident within objects and which therefore has its own independent, objective existence. It exists rather within the human soul (Seele) and has its being as a subjective experience produced in the soul of the individual by an interaction between all the various faculties of the soul and the sense-perceptions which it receives from objects of the external world.[27] The concept of beauty is the highest known to art,[28] and the task of the artist is to convey his subjective experience of the beautiful to his public through the medium of his work of art, in which the beautiful is externalized and objectively represented. He will not, however, achieve this aim by means of the slavish imitation of nature —the prosaic "Abklatschen des Wirklichen" is expressly ruled out.[29] Art, says Grillparzer, is rather a transfigured image (verklärtes Abbild) of nature;[30] it depends upon an intensification of reality (Steigerung des Wirklichen), which is achieved not by the portrayal of nature as it really is, but by the idealization of nature.[31] In this way he reaches the conclusion—far removed from the thinking of the Naturalists—that art in fact consists in "die Hervorbringung einer andern Natur, als die, welche uns umgibt, einer Natur, die mehr mit den Forderungen unsers Verstandes, unserer Empfindung, unsers

Schönheits-Ideals, unsers Strebens nach Einheit übereinstimmt";[32] and truth in art, far from being the "objective" truth of reality as perceived by our cognitive faculty (Erkenntnisvermögen), is rather a subjective, "aesthetic" truth (die *ästhetische* oder *Kunstwahrheit*), which satisfies not merely one part of our being, such as the intellect (Verstand) or the imagination (Phantasie), but all of our faculties—and so gives rise to the experience of the beautiful.[33]

His views on the general problem of the relationship between art and nature and his paramount concern for the beautiful in all art have predictable consequences for Grillparzer's ideas on the particular problem of the dramatic illusion; and here again we find, as we should expect, that he is far from sharing the veristic intention of the Naturalists. He had first addressed himself to the problem of the dramatic illusion in a diary-entry of 1817, posing the question whether the illusion should be absolute or whether the spectator should be conscious that what he is watching is only a fabrication, an imitation of reality. He had decided that the answer lay somewhere between the two possibilities. The spectator must attribute a certain degree of reality to what he sees, otherwise there can be no possibility of his being moved by the tragic emotions of pity and fear. But at the same time he must have a faint, background awareness—almost an unconscious consciousness, as it were—that the drama is in fact an illusion, otherwise art would be indistinguishable from nature with the result that tragedy could only inflict suffering and would afford the spectator none of the aesthetic pleasure (Vergnügen) which is an integral element in our experience of the beautiful and therefore an indispensable requirement of every work of art. The effect of the dramatic illusion may thus be compared to that of a dream:

> Ich stelle mir oft die Wirkung der dramatischen Poesie wie einen Morgentraum, kurz vor dem Aufwachen vor, wo angenehme Bilder um die Stirne gaukeln, uns mit Freude und Schmerz erfüllen, obschon (wenigstens bei mir) immer der Gedanke dazwischen kömmt: es ist ja doch alles nur ein Traum! Aber im nächsten Augenblicke taucht die kaum erwachte Klarheit wieder in die süßen Wellen unter und kommt nur jedesmal, wenn der Eindruck zu stark wird, wieder zum Vorschein.[34]

The adoption in the early 1830s of the term "Gegenwart", used by Goethe in the short theoretical essay *Über epische und dramatische Dichtung* (1797) to define the form of the drama, enabled Grillparzer to restate his ideas on the nature of the dramatic illusion in conceptually clearer, less poetic language, though without in any way materially altering his position.[35] In the important essay *Über den gegenwärtigen Zustand der dramatischen Kunst in Deutschland* (1834)[36] he starts from the premiss that the drama is the strictest of all poetic forms. The lyric and the epic forms "gehen *formell* von einer Wahrheit aus, die dramatische von einer Lüge, und ihre Aufgabe ist, diese Lüge aufrecht zu erhalten, ja sie in letzter Ausbildung zu einer Wahrheit zu machen. Die Lyrik spricht ein Gefühl aus, das Epos erzählt ein Geschehenes (für die Form gleichviel, ob wahr oder erdichtet), das Drama lügt eine Gegenwart." In short, the drama presents us with a semblance of reality which is in fact an illusion. But, Grillparzer argues, the illusion should not be absolute because "eine unabweisliche, zwingende Täuschung würde alle Kunst von vornherein aufheben, eine einschneidendere Wirklichkeit an deren Stelle setzen, und namentlich die Tragödie zu einem Schauspiel für Schlächter und Kannibalen machen"—in other words, an absolute illusion would merely have the effect of destroying the spectator's pleasure and would therefore rob the drama of its beauty. There is, however, a second kind of illusion which is not created solely by the poet through the irresistibly compelling power of his drama but requires the active co-operation of the spectator. The spectator in this case is not expected to accept the dramatic events as fully real. Instead he enters voluntarily into the "supposition" that the drama is "eine *Gegenwart* (ja nicht mit *Wirklichkeit* zu verwechseln)", and this he does subject to the tacit condition that he will reject the supposition if its effects should become too painful for him—i.e. if the poet should present him with scenes so distressing as to destroy the aesthetic pleasure. The essential feature which distinguishes the impression of actuality (Gegenwart) from that of reality (Wirklichkeit) is that the spectator *voluntarily*, and therefore to some extent consciously, co-operates in its creation. By means of this useful distinction Grillparzer is able to explain how the drama can affect us just as powerfully as anything in reality, while yet retaining, in direct contrast to the Naturalists, a clear distinction between the world of art and the world of nature and thus contriving, since the dramatic illusion is not absolute, to safeguard the crucial primacy of the beautiful even in tragedy.

His conviction that the work of art must represent an idealized world of poetic beauty distinct from the world of prosaic reality has further important consequences relevant to our argument, for it governs Grillparzer's attitude to two major questions of form and subject-matter in the drama: the use of verse and the form of the *bürgerliches Trauerspiel*. In both matters he held strong views which separate him radically not only from the Naturalists, but also from the Young Germans and other major writers of the *Vormärz*, and from mid-century Realists like Hebbel or Otto Ludwig. Alone among the leading dramatists of the post-Goethean period in nineteenth-century Germany he will sanction only verse-drama and he utterly rejects the *bürgerliches Trauerspiel*. In the sharpest possible contrast to the Naturalists, who expressly banish verse from the stage as unnatural and unconvincing, Grillparzer argues that precisely because the drama is poetry and not reality, the speech of the dramatic characters should be perceptibly different from the normal speech of reality. Verse, which lies midway between speech and song,[37] is, he believes, the only true poetic mode of expression and therefore the only one which should be employed in the drama. Prose he rules out because it is the language of reality and therefore unpoetic. The strength of his feeling on the subject may be gauged from the tone of what he said to Foglar in a conversation of 1843: "Es ärgert mich, wenn ein guter Dramatiker in Prosa schreibt. . . . Von jeher war der Vers die Sprache der Poesie, und Prosa die der Wirklichkeit. Die Poesie aber will sich eben von der Wirklichkeit entfernen, darum soll sie sich auch im Ausdruck von ihr unterscheiden. . . . Poesie in Prosa ist Unsinn."[38] So strong, in fact, was his dislike of prose that it led him to exclude from the realm of true art the form of the novel, which he regarded at best as "halbe Poesie".[39] He made an exception for only two examples of the genre which he felt could be called truly poetic: *Wilhelm Meister* and *Don Quixote*.[40] And despite being the author of *Der arme Spielmann* he was not happy with the form of the *Novelle* either, for in it he saw "das erste Herabneigen der Poesie zur Prosa".[41]

His explicit rejection of the *bürgerliches Trauerspiel* (and in later life also of the *comédie larmoyante*) is grounded in similar misgivings, though of course the requirement that the drama should be written in verse is in itself enough to rule out this particular genre, since a *bürgerliches Trauerspiel* in verse could for obvious reasons only be ridiculous. The development of the *bürgerliches Trauerspiel* in Germany had been actively encouraged by Lessing, who regarded it as a more realistic form than the high tragedy of the French Classical school and thus more likely to evoke the tragic emotions of pity and fear in a middle-class audience. But it was precisely the realistic aspect of the genre which Grillparzer so disliked, for it seemed to him thoroughly prosaic. He points out that it lacks that idealizing tendency which is a fundamental condition of all poetry[42] and essential if the work of art is to give rise to the experience of the beautiful. Lessing, he believes, has made the mistake of so many aestheticians and allowed his theory, logically developed though it is, to become divorced from the practical realities of art. He writes in 1859-60:

> Gegenwärtig treibt man die metaphysische Ästhetik, Lessing trieb die syllogistische. Von der richtigen Ansicht ausgehend, daß wo die Ursache rätselhaft ist, man die Wirkungen in Auge behalten muß, erkannte er mit Aristoteles Furcht und Mitleid als die Quellen des Wohlgefallens an der Tragödie. Aber nun schloß er logisch weiter. Je mehr Furcht und je mehr Mitleid um so größer die Wirkung. Da nun je näher uns die Personen stehen um so größer der Anteil an ihrem Schicksale sein muß, ergo—und so kam er auf das bürgerliche Trauerspiel und in weiterer Folge das weinerliche Lustspiel: die zwei schlechtesten Gattungen die es gibt.[43]

Given his insistence on the "ideal" aspect of all poetry and his vigorous attacks on the shortcomings of middle-class tragedy (and sentimental comedy), it was inevitable that Grillparzer should find much of the new realistic literature of the nineteenth century thoroughly distasteful. Thus, he despises the dull prosiness of the "Dichter des Wirklich-Wahren", whose obsession with the faithful portrayal of the most trivial minutiae of the narrow little world about them robs their work of any spark of genuine poetry,[44] and he has no patience whatever with the crude, though strident, realism of the Young Germans who are fired by a wretched determination to bring literature closer to the prosaic world of contemporary reality and to press it into the service of wholly unpoetic political and social aims.[45] It is also safe to assume that he cared little for works like Hebbel's *Maria Magdalena*,[46] described by Hebbel himself as a *bürgerliches Trauerspiel*; and it is *a fortiori* certain that he would have detested utterly the stark materialism, the characteristically proletarian settings and the uncompromisingly harsh realism of Naturalist drama.

Further evidence to support the contention that Grillparzer is by no means an advanced Realist is provided by his theoretical remarks on some of the specifically theatrical aspects of the drama. Because he never lost sight of the conviction that the drama does not attempt to reproduce reality exactly as it is and sets out to create the illusion not of reality but of actuality, he did not find it necessary to insist—as the Naturalists, impressed by the example of the Meiningen Court Theatre, were to do—upon a meticulous realism in matters of décor and costume. Provided that the décor and the actors' dress did not actually appear absurd, and so damage the dramatic illusion, he was satisfied.[47] In any case he firmly believed that any attempt to achieve a wholly realistic effect was likely to be self-defeating and merely endanger the illusion which it was intended to strengthen. For this reason he was scathing in his criticism of what he considered to be the over-zealous efforts made in the Burgtheater in the 1860s during the latter years of the Laube era to enhance the authenticity of stage-settings and costumes:

> Je mehr sie sich abmühen, alles haarscharf naturgetreu vorzustellen . . . desto mehr wird die Illusion gestört, ja sie wird zuletzt unmöglich, weil ja doch das Ganze auf Täuschungen beruht, deren Wirklichkeit man nicht herstellen kann. Indem man aber das Bedürfnis nach dieser fehlenden Wirklichkeit immer mehr zu befriedigen trachtet und dadurch immer steigert, indes man alle Nebendinge in Wahrheit umzuwandeln sucht, während man die Hauptsachen doch nicht in Wirklichkeit versetzen kann: die Leute da oben sich doch nicht lieben, heiraten, töten, desto mehr untergräbt man die Wirkung des Ganzen zugunsten des Einzelnen. Und da man mit einem Wort das Spiel nicht zur Wahrheit zu machen vermag, soll man auch nicht suchen durch das Herbeiziehen realistischer Elemente und Nebensachen eine Täuschung zu erhöhen, die doch nur durch die Kunst der Darstellung, durch die Schauspieler, ihren Schwerpunkt findet.[48]

Highly significant are the concluding words of the foregoing quotation, where Grillparzer slips in the opinion that it is not upon elaborate, realistic stage-settings, historically accurate costumes and all the other paraphernalia of the theatre, but upon the competence of the actors, that the dramatic illusion primarily depends.[49] One might have expected (if one did not know him better) that the vital importance which he thus attaches to the function of the actor would lead him to advocate close collaboration, or at least consultation, between poet and actor and make him eager to lend a guiding hand in productions of his own plays. But in fact he never entered into a close working relationship with any theatre and he appears always to have given the theatrical team, performers included, an almost completely free hand.[50] When actors were being recruited for productions of his own works the only point upon which he insisted—in addition to the obvious requirement that every member of the cast must have real acting ability (he knew to his own cost how completely even a good play can be ruined by bad acting)—was that they must all be suited by their physical appearance for the roles which they were to play: "Bei der Rollenverteilung sah ich immer nur darauf, ob ein Schauspieler *äußerlich* das Zeug dazu hatte; wie er dann spielte war seine Sache." In other words, provided that the illusion was not likely to be impaired by an absurd incongruity between the individual's appearance and his role, Grillparzer was content to leave the interpretation of the part to his professional skill as an actor and to refrain from all further intervention.[51]

However, this characteristic reticence in no way prevented him from having some strong views as to what constituted good acting; and the substance of his thinking—which here again diverges from that of the Naturalists as exemplified in the brilliant productions of Otto Brahm at the Freie Bühne and the Deutsches Theater in Berlin—is that the actors should emphatically not set out to create a naturalistic effect. On his visits to the theatre in both Paris and London in 1836 he was forcibly struck by the difference between the style of acting which he encountered there and that which was customarily found at the time in Germany. In Paris he noted that the actors of the Théâtre Français, far from attempting to imitate exactly the behaviour of people in real life, adopted instead a highly stylized manner, the effect of which was to raise their whole performance to an aesthetic plane far above the level of everyday reality: "Es ist als ob man eine Landschaft durch ein gefärbtes Glas betrachtete. Die Luft flammt, die Bäume röteln, alles spielt ins Feurige und Gelbe"; and the result, he felt, compared entirely favourably with the impression of "dull naturalness" normally achieved in the theatres of Germany.[52] In similar vein he commented after a visit to London's Covent Garden Theatre: "Imposant sind die hiesigen besseren Schauspieler. Ich weiß außer der Schröder keinen imposanten Schauspieler in Deutschland. . . . Die Deutschen streben bis zur Unbedeutenheit natürlich zu sein, hier wissen sie wenigstens, daß sie eine Kunst ausüben."[53] His preference for a markedly stylized type of acting is of course in perfect accord with the fundamental principle of his dramatic theory, namely the conviction that the drama is not simply a naturalistically conceived "slice of life" which apes reality in every respect, but an aesthetic production, a work of poetry which strives instead to create the illusion of actuality and so, ultimately, to communicate to the public the artist's subjective experience of perfect beauty.

From time to time critics wishing to emphasize the closeness of Grill-parzer's relationship to the Realists or Naturalists have sought support for their views in other aspects of his works and thought. But their arguments, though not without force, are ultimately not conclusive. It has, for example, been suggested that in at least some of his dramas he shares the Naturalists' determinist view of human behaviour,[54] and it is certainly true that the scope of human freedom as he sees it is very much more restricted than it had been for men of the eighteenth century like Lessing or Schiller;[55] but against this it must be pointed out that his theory of tragedy still clings to the concept of free will.[56] It can also be argued that the unrelieved pessimism which informs his theory of tragedy and is evident in his tragic dramas[57] distances him from the Classical poets and aligns him with the mainstream of nineteenth-century Realist and Naturalist writing; but this argument rests upon the two false assumptions that an unrelieved pessimism is some-thing peculiar to Realism and Naturalism and that all tragic drama of the Realist and Naturalist periods is characterized by a completely hopeless pessimism; it ignores the fact that there is already black pessimism in earlier writers such as Kleist, and a (perhaps rather unexpected) element of optimism in Hebbel's conception of tragedy. Finally, there is the view that he has affinities with the moral relativism typical of so much nineteenth-century writing; but against this Papst makes the telling point that "paradoxical though it may seem to the historian of realism in German literature, Grill-parzer's 'advanced' ethical outlook does not so much point forward to the ethical scepticism and nihilism of nineteenth-century Germany, as indicate a distinctively Austrian, Catholic heritage which has been undermined by the belated rationalism of a Josephinist age."[58] Clearly, the weight of evidence in arguments like these is so finely balanced that they strengthen the case neither of those who are at pains to stress Grillparzer's proximity to the more advanced Realists nor of those who would deny it.

To what general conclusion about Grillparzer's place in the evolution of German literature are we now justified in coming? Let it be said first that we do well to heed the warning sounded by more than one critic that it is as easy as it is foolish to insist too exclusively upon his affinities with any of the major traditions with which he has ties. The truth is that his historical position is unique, for alone among the major German writers he looks both backwards to the traditions of the Classical period and the Austrian Baroque and forward to the coming Realism of the nineteenth century. In so far as he fuses together elements of all three traditions it is perfectly legitimate to describe him as a transitional figure, though the word "transitional" is perhaps less than ideal, for it too readily takes on unfortunate negative connotations and wrongly implies that he is merely a minor figure, uncertain of his own identity and direction, unhappily suspended between various major traditions to each of which he is related but to none of which he ultimately belongs. To classify him as *Biedermeier* is no more satisfactory, partly because of the failure of critical opinion to agree on the meaning of the term and partly because Grillparzer has an awkward way of refusing to conform in one respect or another to the various definitions of it that have so far been attempted. It therefore seems preferable, at least until we have a generally accepted definition of it to which he clearly conforms (assuming that we ever shall), to employ a different classification altogether.[59] And, as was indicated at the beginning of this essay, the evidence of his theory no less than that of his dramatic practice suggests strongly that for clarity, simplicity and accuracy there is no way more appropriate to describe him than as an early Realist, one who in his formative years progressively moves away from his Classical and Baroque antecedents and develops new realistic tendencies, but who is still perceptibly distant from the full-blown Realism of the middle and later decades of the nineteenth century and very far indeed from the Naturalism of the 1880s and 1890s.

W. N. B. MULLAN

St Andrews

NOTES

[1] It is pressed most vigorously in Gundolf's notorious essay, "Franz Grillparzer", *Jahrbuch des Freien Deutschen Hochstifts*, Halle, 1933, pp. 9-93.

[2] A. Sauer, *Einleitung zur fünften Ausgabe Grillparzers Sämtlicher Werke*, Stuttgart, 1892; E. Reich, *Franz Grillparzers Dramen*, Dresden, 1894 (published in a new edition under the title *Grillparzers dramatisches Werk*, Wien, 1938); F. Strich, *Franz Grillparzers Ästhetik*, Berlin, 1905, especially pp. 130-1, 236.

[3] M. Enzinger, *Die Entwicklung des Wiener Theaters vom 16. zum 19. Jahrhundert*, 2 Bde, Berlin, 1918/1919, and "Franz Grillparzer und das Wiener Volkstheater", *Grillparzer-Studien*, hrsg. von O. Katann, Wien, 1924, pp. 9-39; E. Alker, *Franz Grillparzer. Ein Kampf um Leben und Kunst*, Marburg, 1930; G. Baumann, *Franz Grillparzer. Dichtung und österreichische Geistesverfassung*, Frankfurt/Main, 1966.

[4] See, for example, Strich, op. cit., pp. 232-3; F. Sengle, *Das deutsche Geschichtsdrama. Geschichte eines literarischen Mythos*, Stuttgart, 1952, p. 99; J. Kaiser, *Grillparzers dramatischer Stil*, München, 1961, p. 99.

[5] U. Fülleborn, *Das dramatische Geschehen im Werk Franz Grillparzers*, München, 1966, p. 310.

[6] The first chapter of Fülleborn's book contains a useful survey of the alignment of critical opinion on the subject.

[7] See, for example, Gundolf, op. cit., pp. 48-9, 60, 72, 90; Reich, *Grillparzers dramatisches Werk*, pp. 151-3, 160, 350, 353, 357-8; R. Roth, "Grillparzer als Dramaturg", Diss., Frankfurt-am-Main, 1947, pp. 57, 77-8, 83, 97; F. Lorenz, "Die Szene bei Grillparzer", *Grillparzer-Forum Forchtenstein* II (1966), 54.

[8] See, for example, A. D. Klarmann, "Grillparzer und die Moderne", *Das Neue Reich*, 1956, pp. 137-52, and "Psychological Motivation in Grillparzer's *Sappho*", *Monatshefte für deutschen Unterricht* XL (1948), 271-8.

[9] One may of course share Fülleborn's conclusion that he is most appropriately assigned to the period of early Realism without sharing unreservedly all of Fülleborn's arguments and their implications.

[10] Grillparzer, *Sämtliche Werke* [hereafter referred to as *SW*], hrsg. von August Sauer und Reinhold Backmann, Wien, 1909-48, Abt. II, 11, p. 132, Tgb. 3882: "Die Jugendeindrücke wird man nicht los. Meinen eigenen Arbeiten merkt man an, daß ich in der Kindheit mich an den Geister- und Feen-Märchen des Leopoldstädter Theaters ergötzt habe".

[11] Enzinger, "Franz Grillparzer und das Wiener Volkstheater", especially pp. 15, 39.

[12] Grillparzer himself placed the play—certainly in its original version, before the changes suggested by Schreyvogel were made—in the category of the ghost-play, a long-established form of the *Volksstück* (*SW* I, 16, p. 122). Cf. *Grillparzers Gespräche*, hrsg. von August Sauer, 1904-41, I, No. 12, p. 233.

[13] Enzinger, "Franz Grillparzer und das Wiener Volkstheater", pp. 24-5.

[14] *SW* I, 16, pp. 134-5.

[15] Gespr. III, No. 880, pp. 371-2; *SW* I, 16, p. 127.

[16] In fact he had even hesitated to write *Die Ahnfrau* at all because he felt the subject-matter was suitable only for the popular stage and would thus cause his name to be associated with a class of dramatists most of whom he had by this time grown to despise (*SW* I, 16, p. 118).

[17] *SW* II, 8, pp. 296-7, Tgb. 1626.

[18] *SW* II, 8, p. 335, Tgb. 1709; *SW* II, 9, p. 25, Tgb. 1893.

[19] *SW* I, 16, p. 168.

[20] Gespr. III, No. 759, p. 235: "Der dramatische Dichter *soll* nach Effekt ringen".

[21] *SW* I, 16, p. 214.

[22] *SW* II, 8, p. 296, Tgb. 1626. His criticism of Goethe applies only to Goethe's Classical dramas which he considered dramatically and theatrically extremely weak (*SW* II, 7, p. 106, Tgb. 225).

[23] *SW* I, 14, p. 30.

[24] The ghost makes its entry in the suitably ominous setting of the Gothic hall of the Borotins' castle during a storm on a cold, dark winter's night; and the old legend of the ancestral ghost as told by Günther in Act I is clearly intended as a further means of heightening its credibility. Cf. Gespr. III, No. 868, p. 359, where Adolf Foglar records Grillparzer's own words: "Wenn eine Ahnfrau erscheint, so muß ich's den Leuten glaublich gemacht haben, daß eine Ahnfrau erscheinen kann".

[25] The characters most frequently adduced in support of the claim are Bancbanus and Otto von Meran in *Ein Treuer Diener seines Herrn* and Kaiser Rudolf II in *Ein Bruderzwist in Habsburg*. See the views of Gundolf etc., referred to in Note 7 above.

[26] It is worth noting in passing that Grillparzer is similarly far removed from the drastic truth to nature or reality demanded by Büchner in *Lenz* or in the letter to his family of 28 July 1835. He is even considerably distant from the more modest realism to which Fontane, for example, gives his blessing at various points in his writings (including *Unsere lyrische und epische Poesie seit 1848*, his reviews of Kielland's *Arbeiter* and Hauptmann's *Vor Sonnenaufgang* and his discussion, first published posthumously in *Gesammelte Werke*, Berlin, 1905-11, 2nd Series, IX, of Lindau's *Der Zug nach dem Westen*). He is closer to the "poetic realism" or "artistic realism" which Otto Ludwig labours to define, in sometimes rather vague language, in his *Studien*.

[27] At the same time, however, any object—such as a work of art—which gives rise to this experience is described as beautiful. For a full account of the large and complex question of Grillparzer's conception of beauty see Strich, op. cit., or my own unpublished B.Litt. dissertation, *Grillparzer's aesthetic theory with special reference to his conception of the drama as "eine Gegenwart"*, Oxford, 1973.

[28] "deren oberster Begriff" (*SW* I, 14, p. 8).

[29] *SW* II, 7, p. 335, Tgb. 879; *SW* II, 11, p. 195, Tgb. 4023.

[30] *SW* II, 8, p. 95, Tgb. 1232.

[31] *SW* I, 13, p. 136; *SW* II, 7, p. 233, Tgb. 581.

[32] *SW* II, 7, p. 279, Tgb. 733.

[33] *SW* II, 7, p. 345, Tgb. 890.

[34] *SW* II, 7, p. 110, Tgb. 240. Cf. *SW* II, 7, p. 234, Tgb. 585.

[35] Grillparzer's conception of the drama as "eine Gegenwart" is the central, unifying idea in his whole dramatic theory. For full details see either my own dissertation, which deals with the subject in depth, or Strich, op. cit., especially pp. 89 ff.

[36] *SW* I, 14, pp. 72 ff.

[37] *SW* II, 11, p. 256, Tgb. 4105.

[38] Gespr. III, No. 800, p. 274.

[39] Gespr. III, No. 800, p. 274; *SW* II, 9, p. 156, Tgb. 2137.

[40] Gespr. III, No. 847, p. 340.

[41] *SW* II, 10, p. 286, Tgb. 3476.

[42] *SW* II, 7, p. 120, Tgb. 258.

[43] *SW* II, 12, p. 36, Tgb. 4256. Cf. *SW* II, 11, pp. 214-15, Tgb. 4040; *SW* II, 11, p. 223, Tgb. 4050. It is not fortuitous that not one of Grillparzer's own major dramas has a realistic setting in the contemporary world. Some of them have a historical or legendary background, some have a mythological setting, while others are cast in the fanciful mould of the *Zauberstück*; and all of them are written in verse, albeit verse which is closer than that of the Classicists to the patterns of normal speech. He has therefore in every case made a deliberate effort to avoid coming too close to everyday life. Faithful to his theory, he spares no pains to make his plays theatrically effective so that they impress the spectator as "Gegenwart"; yet they do not descend from their (sometimes more, sometimes less) elevated poetic plane to the level of common "Wirklichkeit".

[44] *SW* I, 14, p. 166. See also *SW* I, 11, p. 255, No. 327, where he names Iffland specifically. Cf. his caustic epigram directed against Freytag's prosy *Soll und Haben* which, in the celebrated words of Julian Schmidt, portrays "das deutsche Volk . . ., wo es in seiner Tüchtigkeit zu finden ist, nämlich bei seiner Arbeit" (*SW* I, 12/1, p. 268, No. 1427).

[45] *SW* II, 9, p. 354, Tgb. 2856; *SW* I, 14, pp. 163-4.

[46] Although he never actually mentions *Maria Magdalena* specifically, one may see an implied rejection of this kind of play in a general criticism which he makes of Hebbel: "Übrigens mißfiel mir immer die Wahl seiner Stoffe. Er erfreute sich an dem Verzerrten, an den Schattenseiten des Lebens, und die Verwickelung, nicht die Lösung war sein Element. Bei aller Großartigkeit und Kraft seiner Darstellung hat es ihm doch an dem Ideal wahrer Anmut und Schönheit gefehlt" (Gespr. V, No. 1208, p. 230).

[47] Gespr. V, No. 1182, p. 128. He insists only "daß nicht Unsinn und Lächerlichkeiten durch Vernachlässigung der Nebendinge entstehen". As an example of an inadequate setting which did damage the illusion we may quote the case of the open-air theatre which he once visited in Preßburg (*SW* II, 11, p. 24, Tgb. 3633).

[48] Gespr. V, No. 1182, pp. 126-8.

[49] His opinion is reflected in the nature of his own stage-directions, for, as Kaiser (op. cit., p. 84) observes, these are concerned far more frequently with the precise prescription of the movements and gestures of the actors than with questions of décor and costume, which he clearly considered less important.

[50] Gespr. VI, No. 1531, VII, p. 278.

[51] Gespr. III, No. 838, p. 335. Cf. Gespr. VI, No. 1528, p. 269; *SW* I, 16, p. 160. The example of *Sappho* provides a good illustration of what can go wrong when a major role in a play is taken by an actor or actress of unsuitable appearance (See Gespr. V, No. 1190, pp. 166-8 and p. 173; Laube, "Nachwort zu *Sappho*").

[52] *SW* II, 10, pp. 10-11, Tgb. 2884.

[53] *SW* II, 10, p. 124, Tgb. 3126.

[54] Reich, op. cit., p. 160.

[55] For an account of Grillparzer's attitude towards the question of free will see F. Kainz, *Grillparzer als Denker*, Wien, 1975, pp. 110 ff.

[56] *SW* I, 14, pp. 30-31. For a full account of his theory of tragedy see either my own dissertation, pp. 126 ff., or Strich, op. cit., pp. 183 ff. It should, however, be pointed out that Strich's account is misleading in that it wrongly implies that Grillparzer completely abandons the idea of free will.

[57] In accordance with his theory, Grillparzer's typical hero is spiritually broken by the events which befall him; his heroes do not achieve the sublime dignity which normally surrounds Schiller's heroes, for they do not rise triumphantly above Fate by willing their own downfall and so dying morally free.

[58] E. E. Papst, *Grillparzer: "Des Meeres und der Liebe Wellen"*, London, 1967, p. 18.

[59] Significantly, Fülleborn, op. cit., p. 13, observes that most recent criticism tries to avoid using the term.

IV

NESTROY'S
ZU EBENER ERDE UND ERSTER STOCK:
A REAPPRAISAL

While the interest shown in Nestroy's comedies continues undiminished, the principal areas of investigation remain the question of comedy and the works' relation to theatre history. Relatively little attention has been paid, however, to the *Lokalposse* called *Zu ebener Erde und erster Stock, oder die Launen des Glückes*, which tends to be dealt with too often in general terms or merely referred to in passing, to serve as an example of whatever point is being made,[1] both having the effect of obscuring the relatively complex questions posed by the play in relation to Nestroy's *opus*. Two factors which have tended to militate against a more thorough treatment of the play have been its relative proximity, from a present-day point of view, to the much more widely-known *Lumpazivagabundus*, first performed some two and a half years previously, and the device of the horizontally divided stage, undoubtedly the most immediately obvious feature of the play, but one which has perhaps been given more attention than the content.[2]

Let us start with the technique of the divided stage, if only to assign it its proper role as merely one feature among several, and not the one overriding element in the play. Although Mautner states that Nestroy was not dependent on a previous source for this device,[3] it should be seen as neither more nor less than a development of the baroque stagecraft with its mechanical devices that was still very much in use in the Viennese theatre of Raimund's day and which was used by Nestroy in *Lumpazivagabundus*. Raimund's plays are after all set in two worlds—the world of the spirits and the world of the mortals below or the "niedere Welt" as Hofmannsthal calls it in *Die Frau ohne Schatten*, his own *Zauberstück*. Already, therefore, a horizontal division is implied on the stage, although, being portrayed consecutively not simultaneously, it was not translated into the more specific terms of *Zu ebener Erde*. . . . The fourfold division of the stage in *Das Haus der Temperamente* is another instance of the same technique, for which there is no direct source,[4] although one must suppose that the success of *Zu ebener Erde* . . . influenced Nestroy. What he has done in choosing the device of the divided stage is to appropriate a feature of the baroque and Viennese traditional theatre and to employ it on stage in a de-mythologised manner, translated into social terms, or, in the case of *Das Haus der Temperamente*, into psychological terms.

It is noteworthy that the latter play, from the point of view of characters and plot, is divided essentially into two, both flats on the first floor being linked in all respects (sons, daughters and the fathers' friends) by the love intrigue, and the pattern is identical for the flats on the ground floor. When seen in this way, the essential difference becomes clear, for rather than an interweaving of complementary elements of a single plot, *Das Haus der Temperamente* simply repeats the double action in each flat with only minor variations. O. M. Fontana's comment on both plays that it was Nestroy's principle "ein und dasselbe Geschehen auf verschiedenen Ebenen und von verschiedenen Gesichtspunkten her sichtbar zu machen und sie alle miteinander zu verbinden, so daß die verschiedenen Erlebnisinhalte einander widersprechen, aber auch ergänzen und sich unaufhaltsam in eines zusammenschließen"[5] is therefore totally applicable to neither. The point is surely that in the two plays the identical technique is used for different ends. In *Das Haus der Temperamente*, the division of the stage into four is primarily a device to create comedy by allowing repetition, whereas in *Zu ebener Erde* . . . the divided stage serves the intrigue.

Mautner had in fact little time for this play, calling it "dieses schwächeren der Stücke Nestroys" (*Komödien* I, 574). One is led, however, to wonder why he saw the play in this light. The opinion was obviously not shared by Nestroy's audiences, to whom the play was performed 134 times from its première on 24 September 1835 until 1856, a figure exceeded only by three other of his 83 works.[6] It may perhaps be objected that the development of the play is predictable from the beginning and therefore not of great dramatic merit. Does the fact that a play is obvious imply that it is weak in its construction? One only has to look at Brechtian epic theatre to realise that such is not the case. There is no doubt that much of the impact of *Zu ebener Erde* . . . would be lost without this predictability. "The 'Posse mit Gesang' ", as F. Walla observed in another context, ". . . has its own laws"[7] and, knowing these laws, one expects from the outset that Adolf and Emilie will be united, that the *Tandlerfamilie* will see better days, that Goldfuchs will come to grief, and one is therefore able to concentrate, not on what happens, but on how it is brought about. Indeed, one is inclined to agree with Bauer when he says, "Die besten seiner Stücke laufen ab wie gutfunktionierende Uhrwerke" (p. 330). If the quality of "gutfunktionierende Uhrwerke" is in fact a criterion of merit in Nestroy's works, then we must certainly assign *Zu ebener Erde* . . . a higher place than did Mautner. In the same context it must be added that the clockwork quality of the plot is reflected in Nestroy's masterly control of the divided stage, with its parallel actions and dialogues in contrapuntal patterns.

Another objection possibly implied in Mautner's criticism, and which is perhaps what he had in mind when he wrote of the "etwas blasse, menschenfreundliche Stil des Stückes" (*Komödien* I, 574), is the fact that the play relies heavily on artificial means in order to bring about the desired conclusion. The abrupt changes of fortune of the two families are not motivated and are dependent on outside circumstances: the chance purchase of the Lord's coat, the winning of the lottery prize—an obvious example of pure chance as the identical motif, at Fortuna's instigation, in *Lumpazivagabundus* shows—and Adolf's sudden inheritance on the one hand are matched by the behaviour of Goldfuchs' son, the disastrous outcome of Goldfuchs' speculation and the failure of a bank. The fact that all these disasters are reported rather than portrayed gives them an impersonal quality, beyond the control of the characters on stage. At the end of the play it is made clear that one is to interpret these changes as being caused purely by chance:

'''
's Glück treibt's auf Erden gar bunt,
's Glück bleibt halt stets kugelrund.[8]
'''

In other words, Nestroy has not attempted to justify the changes but has again followed a well-established Viennese tradition, with the difference that the Fortuna-motif has been de-mythologised by the absence of an actual Fortuna figure on stage. It would be wrong therefore to judge the play by the demands of a more sophisticated and realistic theatre and hence one can hardly accuse Nestroy of writing a weak play merely because he adhered to a popular tradition, a tradition to which he continued to adhere in subsequent, more widely acclaimed plays, where the conclusion is brought about by equally improbable means. One has only to think of *Der Talisman* or *Einen Jux will er sich machen* where Nestroy's awareness that he is following tradition is only too clear: "was 's Jahr Onkel und Tanten sterben müssen, bloß damit alles gut ausgeht—!" (*GW* III, 700 [IV, x])

The relationship to Viennese tradition has further given rise to misleading analyses of the play, largely because it was written only two and a half years after *Lumpazivagabundus* and was the next better-known play which Nestroy wrote after the great success of *Lumpazivagabundus*. This proximity, together with a certain similarity in the abrupt changes of fortune, have caused critics to place *Zu ebener Erde* . . . in the same category as *Lumpazivagabundus*.[9] The similarity between the two plays appears at first sight to be strong, particularly when one considers the final scene of each. Bauer describes them, in speaking of Nestroy's early plays in general, as "eine Pirouette des Autors, die wohl vom ganzen damaligen Publikum—oft mit Überraschung—als solche verstanden wurde" (p. 332). Accordingly the play is to be interpreted as an example of Nestroy's cynical treatment of tradition, and of his "Umkehr und parodistische Verneinung des biedermeierlichen Weltbilds seiner Vorgänger" (Bauer, p. 331), while at the same time apparently conforming outwardly to tradition. There are, however, a number of objections which must be raised against applying such an interpretation to *Zu ebener Erde* . . . .

An analysis of the element of chance will show the diversity of the two plays. To begin with, there is no element of a test in *Zu ebener Erde* . . ., unlike the situation in *Lumpazivagabundus* where Fortuna's intervention is designed to illustrate the power-structure of the *Feenwelt*. In our play the lack of a test motif also removes questions of moral or ethical superiority where an external agency is required to bring about a specified outcome, as is the case in many of Raimund's plays. Fortuna is not therefore to be seen as an instrument of justice (at least not in bringing about the improvement in the fortunes of the Schlucker family) nor as a means of restoring social order. In fact it is the mention of an abstract force of chance in the last scene which takes much of the element of social comment out of the play and enables it to be seen to adhere to the social assumption of the day. On the other hand the last scene is not in contrast to the previous action, but is a direct consequence of it and has been anticipated by previous events.

Again there is no suggestion that Fortuna is directly concerned in the love intrigue, in the sense that Fortuna intervenes specifically to bring about a union of the lovers which would otherwise have been impossible. It is true that Adolf's unexpected good fortune makes the situation considerably easier for the couple, but they had already made plans—albeit incomplete and conventional—for an elopement. Here again one may interpret the Fortuna element as a means by which Nestroy is able to adhere to social conventions in that Adolf's new-found wealth absolves the couple from the necessity of an elopement, which in itself implies a defiance of parental authority. Nestroy is therefore able to avoid the dilemma of having to portray a direct clash between the two conventions, both of which are approved of by society, and having to decide on the victory of one over the other.

Since there is no actual Fortuna figure on stage in this play, the element of chance is not discussed on stage in the manner of *Lumpazivagabundus*, where the reasons for her intervention are clearly specified at the beginning. Hence it is not possible for the audience to be spectators of an intervention which is specifically designed to realise certain previously defined aims. In the case of *Lumpazivagabundus*, the audience's awareness of these aims gave the intervention of Fortuna an ethical purpose, which ultimately turns out to be unethical, since the triumph of true love can only be brought about by the triumph of *Liederlichkeit*. For this reason one must draw the conclusion that the role of chance in *Zu ebener Erde . . .* cannot be used to discredit the *genre* as it was in *Lumpazivagabundus*, nor does it oblige the playwright to provide a totally artificial ending in order to appear to uphold convention. Hence this play lies outside Sengle's generalisation that: "Nestroy, der gewiß die Kehrseite der Gemütlichkeit sah, versäumt es nicht, sich mit Hilfe biedermeierlicher Rahmenhandlungen an den herrschenden Geist anzupassen" (I, 112), a comment which clearly applies to *Einen Jux will er sich machen* or particularly to such early plays as *Lumpazivagabundus* or *Weder Lorbeerbaum noch Bettelstab*. As has been shown in examining the treatment of the Fortuna-motif, *Zu ebener Erde . . .*, on the other hand, can be said to adhere to the spirit of the time, without an artificial ending or any other form of "Rahmenhandlung", since the assumptions of the play and the progress of the plot throughout the play lead logically to the conclusion actually given.

The presence of the Fortuna-motif leads us to question another commonly-held view of the play, namely the tendency to link it with the *Besserungs-stück*. As the play is not a *Zauberstück* it should not strictly be termed a *Besserungsstück*, but it has several times been included in, or considered together with, this category.[10] The play, it is true, has features similar to that of the *Besserungsstück*, particularly its cyclical structure with the motif of " 's Glück is kugelrund"[11] and in Nestroy's plans for the rehabilitation of Goldfuchs and Johann (see below). Goldfuchs, although scarcely the central figure, is nevertheless the one who, by his downfall, is the most obvious candidate for the process of self-realisation and improvement. His final words in the play, however, are:

(*zu Adolf und Emilien, deren Hände er zusammenlegt*):
Nehmt meinen besten Segen!—Mein Beispiel gebe
warnend euch die Lehre: Fortunas Gunst ist wandelbar.

(*GW* II, 549 [III, xxxii])

These words, as can be seen from the stage directions, are to be taken as part of the final tableau and as such are intended more for the audience than for the characters involved, giving an apparent summing-up of the impact of the play. At first sight the phrase "Mein Beispiel gebe warnend euch die Lehre" could be taken as being within the tradition of the *Besserungsstück*, and perhaps was an attempt to this end on the part of Nestroy himself. The rest of the sentence, however, immediately negates this impression, since, if Fortuna is capricious, how can Goldfuchs' disasters be an example to others? And since this is the only insight which Goldfuchs achieves, it can hardly be said that he has come to realise his own faults with a view to remedying them. Similarly the evidence is lacking that Goldfuchs has been forced to come to terms with his changed situation and to resume life according to new principles, as is the case with the central characters of *Lumpazi-vagabundus* or of *Müller, Kohlenbrenner und Sesseltrager*, where the three-fold lapse of time is central to both the plot and significance of the play. In addition, Goldfuchs has his virtues which are discernible even before the catastrophe, particularly in his reaction to his son's follies, so that the final scenes can scarcely be said to portray a true change of character. The element of *Besserung* is therefore quite lacking in *Zu ebener Erde* . . . .

In that case could it be said that, after all, the play parodies the *Besserungsstück* and that the ending is merely a cynical attempt by Nestroy to bring the play to a suitable conclusion? This point of view is certainly implicit in Bauer's opinion that the early plays ended with "eine Pirouette des Autors", but it is equally not the case that, in contradiction to the rest of Bauer's comment, his audiences saw the ending of this particular play as such. The *Wiener Theaterzeitung* of 30 September 1835 commented on the play with the words: "Es ist seit langen Jahren auf den Volksbühnen kein Stück erschienen, das sich an Keuschhaftigkeit . . . mit diesem messen könnte."[12] Parody is largely a question of degree and, although *Zu ebener*

Erde . . . has much that is illogical and artificial in its plot, it shares these features with the majority of Nestroy's plays. In terms of the Viennese Popular Theatre this play does in fact have a plot which leads naturally to its conclusion, unlike such deliberate parodies as *Lumpazivagabundus* or *Weder Lorbeerbaum noch Bettelstab.*

It could also be objected that the love intrigue, with all the traditional elements of parental opposition, secret meetings and planned elopements, is meant to have the effect of parody. On the other hand all these traditional elements are precisely that and no more, just as is the eventual happy ending. In this play there is no hint that these elements are to be taken at anything other than their face value, unlike, for instance, *Einen Jux will er sich machen* with Marie's automatic "das schickt sich nicht" whenever any of the stock elements are mentioned. The love intrigue in fact plays a considerable part in enabling social convention to survive the upheavals of the third act, since Emilie is no longer faced with marrying beneath herself for love but can look forward to a love match with her social equal, if not superior. Hence far from superficially resolving conflicts by an imposed ending, Nestroy is able in the obligatory happy ending to combine the upholding of social convention with the demands of romantic love.

When one examines the characters, it is certainly the case that Johann, Damian and Christoph all exhibit features which anticipate, in their verbal comedy and attitudes to life, later Nestroy characters, and yet at the same time all three stand apart from the plot of the play, in which they have little real significance, unlike Knieriem, Lorenz (in *Die verhängnisvolle Faschingsnacht*) or Titus Feuerfuchs. Paradoxically it is in the figure of Johann that we have yet another example to show that this play is not as similar to *Lumpazivagabundus* or as typical of Nestroy's works in general as one might suppose. Johann is an intriguer, playing on the weakness and follies of others, as do many of the other characters played by Nestroy himself. At the same time this nature springs from a well-defined view of life and of the aims he expects to achieve, witness his objections to marriage:

> Der Ehstand, wenn er kinderlos is, is um fünfzig Prozent kostspieliger als der ledige; kommt Familie so steigt es auf hundert Prozent; (*GW* II, 488 [II, xvi])

and to gambling:

> Man verliert Geld und Zeit. Zeitverlust ist auch Geldverlust, also verliert man doppeltes Geld und kann nur einfaches gewinnen. (*GW* II, 494 [[II, xxi])

In the play itself Johann's role is one of dishonest dealings, rather than one of superiority over the other characters which Titus Feuerfuchs displays by his wit. There is a further difference in the fact that, while both are able to manipulate their surroundings to their own advantage, in Titus' case this has the effect of exposing a number of weaknesses and pretensions in the other characters. Johann, however, cannot be said to expose his master's weaknesses since these are made sufficiently evident at other points in the play, nor can his dishonest dealings serve solely as an example of the dangers to which Goldfuchs exposes himself by his weakness since the minor figure of the cook Meridon also takes advantage of his master in the same way. Hence such action has much more the effect of exposing Johann's own fundamentally dishonest character.

It may be objected that the other Nestroy roles in the earlier plays are also not intended to display the weakness of other characters. One reason for this is the fact that the traits of these characters are sufficiently clear without such a figure, as is the case in *Das Haus der Temperamente*. Nevertheless, Johann and Schlankel can be clearly distinguished in that the latter's role is obviously central to the plot as a whole. The basis for their intrigues is also greatly different. Schlankel is motivated by a wish to be in a position of control over events, also taking the form of *schadenfreude*. In Johann's case, motivation is purely material. The figure of Johann cannot therefore be said to contribute to any establishment of a morally superior element in the play by his "Schärfe des Blicks und verblüffende Sicherheit des Auftretens".[13] That his dishonesty subsequently leads to an undignified downfall must prevent us from placing him in the same category as Titus Feuerfuchs or even Knieriem, the latter being at least partially excused by his fatalistic belief in the comet, an unworldly element quite lacking in Johann, and which on the surface enables Nestroy to motivate his rehabilitation: "Ist das ein Glück, Weib, der Komet is aus'blieb'n" (*GW* I, 640 [III, xvii]).

That Nestroy did in fact write additional scenes involving, amongst other things, the rehabilitation of Johann and his marriage to Fanny,[14] implies that at one stage he felt the need to make the play adhere even more closely to prevailing opinions. As it is, even without this additional material, it must be said that the treatment of Johann differs widely from that of similar figures in Nestroy's other works, to the extent that, far from being a means of attacking Biedermeier assumptions, Johann becomes a means of strengthening these very assumptions. In referring to the alternative ending, Rommel wrote: "Es handelt sich bei solchen Planungen um mehr als bloß ein Happy-End" (*GW* II, 729), implying that the re-establishment of the situation at the beginning of the play (including Goldfuchs upstairs, the Schluckers below) was an expression of a wish or need on Nestroy's part to make the play comply with the traditions of his age. If this is so, why did this particular ending not become the definitive one? The answer is surely that it did not prove necessary, for, even without it, this is the play in which Nestroy comes closest to the Biedermeier spirit in so many of its aspects.

Although *Zu ebener Erde* . . . aroused, in contemporary critics, hopes that their wish for a move towards the treatment of social themes in the Viennese popular comedy was being fulfilled (see *GW* I, 82-88), there are a number of significant features in this play which differ from Nestroy's later treatment of social themes. Goldfuchs apparently believes that his wealth is inexhaustible and acts accordingly, comedy being created by the incongruity of his attitude towards money as well as by the intrigues of Johann with his master's money. Goldfuchs does not share the vulgarity or self-conscious attitude towards wealth of the *nouveaux riches* Fett (in *Liebesgeschichten und Heiratssachen*) and Zwirn, and similarly his plans for his daughter are motivated by a wish for financial consolidation rather than for social advancement. At the same time the element of "Kleider machen Leute", satirised in the figure of the landlord in *Liebesgeschichten und Heiratssachen*, is largely lacking in *Zu ebener Erde* . . . . One must conclude, therefore, that the social element in this play is, in many respects, a continuation of Raimund's approach in *Der Verschwender* or *Der Bauer als Millionär* rather than a fore-runner of the more radical treatment of the theme in Nestroy's later work.

It is perhaps the supreme paradox of *Zu ebener Erde* . . . that, once Nestroy had freed himself from the magical externals of the *Geisterwelt* in the *Wiener Volkskomödie* tradition, he was able to produce a work that conformed most nearly to the spirit of the same tradition. Seen in this light, the play takes on its true perspective in the overall development of Nestroy's work. He was able to see through the tradition within which he had been working and grasp its essential characteristics, including them in his work in a secularised context, but without discarding those external features which lent themselves to his own preferences in the choice of material and techniques for his comedies. At the same time Nestroy's further development is anticipated in the figure of Johann, whose successors are truly integrated in the plot of later works, as well as in the plot itself which, far-fetched and illogical though it may be, nevertheless has an ending that is a consequence of what has gone before, not a mere "Pirouette" tacked on to satisfy the public's expectations and the playwright's cynicism.

The play therefore represents a transitional phase of Nestroy's work and as such is difficult to place neatly in given categories. It should instead be considered first as a separate entity and the full nature of the various elements in the play dealt with within the context of the play itself. Comparisons with other plays of Nestroy tend to show a contrast rather than a similarity and hence illustrate the misleading nature of the tendency to deal with the play by making passing reference to it as one example among several.

Wit, mastery of the stage, acceptance of tradition and yet a critical outlook, all are there in *Zu ebener Erde* . . ., a play which, in O. M. Fontana's words, gives us "den ganzen Nestroy" (p. 906).

P. M. POTTER

Ife, Nigeria

NOTES

[1] For examples, see Friedrich Sengle, *Biedermeierzeit* (Stuttgart, 1971), I, 187 and Roger Bauer, "Johann Nestroy" in Benno von Wiese, ed., *Deutsche Dichter des 19. Jahrhunderts* (Berlin, 1969), pp. 332, 334.

[2] E.g. Gertrud Seidmann, "Johann Nestroy" in Alex Nathan, ed., *German Men of Letters* (London, 1969), Vol. V and Ernst Alker, *Die deutsche Literatur im 19. Jahrhundert* (Stuttgart, 1969).

[3] Franz H. Mautner, ed., Johann Nestroy, *Komödien* (Frankfurt, 1970), I, 574, hereafter referred to as *Komödien*.

[4] Cf. Otto Basil, *Nestroy* (Reinbek bei Hamburg, 1967), p. 95.

[5] Oskar Maurus Fontana, "Johann Nestroy: Leben und Werk" in Johann Nestroy. *Werke* (München, 1968), pp. 908 f.

[6] The number of performances for each play is given in Johann Nestroy, *Gesammelte Werke*, ed. Otto Rommel (Wien, 1948-1949), I, 190-193.

[7] " 'Fiktion' and 'Fiktionsbruch' in the Comedies of Nestroy", *GLL* XXVI (Oct. 1972), 14.

[8] *Gesammelte Werke*, II, 549 [III, xxxii]. *Zu ebener Erde* . . . is to be found in vol. II of the *Gesammelte Werke* (hereafter referred to as *GW*), pp. 425-549. All subsequent quotations from Nestroy's works are from this edition, the act and scene numbers being given in square brackets.

[9] See Otto Rommel, "Johann Nestroy, der Satiriker auf der Altwiener Komödienbühne", in *GW*, I, 87 f., or the chronological classification in Bauer, pp. 330 f. which implies that *Zu ebener Erde* . . . is to be included in the earliest, or "kolossalisch", period.

[10] Sengle, I, 187; Basil, p. 91; and by implication in Walter Dieze, "Tradition und Ursprünglichkeit in den 'Besserungsstücken' des Wiener Volkstheaters", *Akten des III. internationalen Germanistenkongresses* (Amsterdam, 1965), p. 185; Rommel in Johann Nestroy, *Der Zerissene* (Stuttgart, 1959), p. 81.

[11] See W. E. Yates, *Nestroy, Satire and Parody in Viennese Popular Comedy* (Cambridge, 1972), p. 171 and W. E. Yates, " 'Die Jugendeindrücke wird man nicht los . . .' Grillparzer's Relation to the Viennese Popular Theatre", *GR* XLVIII (March 1973), 137.

[12] Quoted in *Komödien*, I, 574.

[13] Franz H. Mautner, "Nestroy: *Der Talisman*" in Benno von Wiese, ed., *Das deutsche Drama* (Düsseldorf, 1968), II, 29.

[14] For a summary of the contents of this now lost MS, see *GW*, II, 728 f.

V

THE USE OF LEITMOTIFS
IN STIFTER'S *BRIGITTA*

"Selbst seine Wiederholungen werden ihm nur bey gewöhnlichen Lesern Abbruch thun, weil sie in der allmäligen Entfaltung der inneren Anschauung liegend, in der Entwicklung der Novelle unentbehrlich und gleichsam noth-wendig erscheinen . . .". This excerpt from a contemporary review[1] of *Gedenke mein! Taschenbuch für 1844*, in which the original version of *Brigitta* was first published, suggests that early readers were not unaware of Stifter's use of repetition as a stylistic device. This aspect of his craft, by no means confined to *Brigitta* but strongly represented in it, has not received much attention from critics. In this article I want to consider examples of Stifter's use of leitmotifs; I shall refer mainly to the revised text of 1846 that was published in volume 4 of *Studien* in 1847,[2] but shall also use the original *Gedenke mein!* text.[3]

Various commentators have mentioned aspects of the differences that Stifter introduced when revising *Brigitta*, though without either using the fruits of detailed comparison to explain problematic passages in the final version, or considering the pattern of verbal and conceptual repetitions. Let us take a brief look at the first of these matters, before studying the second in some detail. Whereas in most respects the later version of *Brigitta* is an extension of the earlier, the philosophical introduction is much longer in the first version and, in keeping with the general tenor, also much more romantic. Deletion of the phrase "Wir . . . verspritzen unser Blut für ihn—und wissen nicht warum" (Uf, 182) from the *Studienfassung* leaves suspended and un-explained the reference to Brigitta's tears over the picture of a brother sacrificing himself for another (Sf, 204; Uf, 210).

Characteristic of the first versions of Stifter's stories is the use of long, involved sentence-structures, with usually short sense-units separated from each other by an assortment of single and double dashes, commas, or occasion-ally semicolons; by comparison with the revised versions, the earlier ones contain far more loan-words. A striking example of Stifter's approach to the task of rewriting is provided by comparison between the two versions of the passage in which the narrator describes his first impressions of the Major. In the *Urfassung* the sentence that begins "Er war damals in allen Gesellschaften gefeiert . . ." (Uf, 185) extends to more than a page of text; in the *Studienfassung* the content of this sentence is little altered beyond the removal of references to the Major's almost supernatural powers, but it is now spread over no fewer than eleven sentences (Sf, 167-8).

A good example of Stifter's later expansion of material is provided by the passage early in the second section of *Brigitta* that follows the description of the sunset (Uf, 198-9; Sf, 183-90). Two paragraphs in the *Urfassung*, a six-line-long reflection and a 30-line-long speech, are expanded to seven and a half pages. More revealing than the changes in the paragraph of direct speech, which is comparatively little altered, is the rewriting of the short paragraph in such a way that each of its elements is incorporated in the final version, though with differing emphases and in a slightly different order. This can perhaps best be illustrated by referring the reader after each phrase of the *Urfassung* (Uf, 198) to the relevant page in the *Studienfassung*.

> Und so ritten wir am andern Tage wieder herum [Wir ritten heute nicht mehr so im Allgemeinen herum—Sf, 184], und ehe acht vergangen waren [Da ich einmal längere Zeit auf der Besitzung des Majors war, da ich die Teile derselben übersah, und verstehen lernte, da die Dinge vor mir wuchsen und ich an dem Gedeihen derselben Anteil nahm: —Sf, 190], hatte mich das gleichförmig sanfte Abfließen dieser Tage und Geschäfte so eingesponnen, daß ich mich wohl und ebenmäßig angeregt fühlte [Sf, 190—no changes], und auf all den Trödel unserer Städte als ein viel zu Kleines vergaß [und auf unsere Städte vergaß, gleichsam als wäre das ein Kleines, was in ihnen bewegt wird —Sf, 190]. Mir fielen oft die alten starken Römer ein, die den Landbau so liebten [Die Einsamkeit und Kraft dieser Beschäftigungen erinnerte mich häufig an die altern starken Römer, die den Landbau auch so sehr geliebt hatten . . . —Sf, 190, two paragraphs earlier than the three preceding linked quotations].

Although the gain in knowledge of the Major's idyllic achievement is of greater scope and consequence than the losses, it is significant for the motivation of the story that when revising the paragraph containing the Major's revelations about his nation's and his own past (Uf, 198; Sf, 189), Stifter omits mention of the Major's debt to a woman for the example he now follows in improving his lands and working with his people. Similarly, Stifter shortly after again makes less obvious the Major's past relationship to the woman whom we may only from this point identify as Brigitta Maroshely. The first version juxtaposed rather clumsily the ugly young girl's portrait in the Major's writing-room with the suddenly announced first visit to Marosheli (Uf, 201; Sf, 192-4). Although suspense is hardly increased in the revised version (Brigitta is the only woman to appear in the first two chapters), it is artistically and psychologically more satisfying.

Recognition of the importance of recurrent words and ideas in *Brigitta* is not new. The writer who has contributed more than any other to our awareness of this device is Ernst Feise, who in an apparently little-known chapter of his book *Xenion*[4] draws attention to certain of the often-used words, and attempts to link them with characters in the story. The evidence does not on the whole justify his findings, but the article deserves attention as an early study of a prominent but neglected feature of Stifter's art. Feise is too neat in his categorizing. He sees each of the three main characters as depicted by a single symbolic word: the Major by "das Ziel", Brigitta by

"Schönheit", and the narrator by "das Auge".[5] Attractive as the idea might seem, it does not work out in practice. We shall consider "Ziel" shortly. Neither "Auge" nor "Schönheit" is applied to only one character; both words are too commonly used for there to be the possibility of a consistent and conscious application limited to the special significance that Feise favours. He is also unconvincing in his contention that Fate steps in four times in *Brigitta*, once in each chapter[6]—a point that can be refuted on the evidence of the text.[7]

Stifter has suffered more than most writers from critics who see what they want to see in his works, who ignore points that run counter to their theories. Even a commentator with the perception of Konrad Steffen[8] does not escape the danger: from the justifiable suggestion that the Major is "innerlich einsam . . . und glutvoll wie die Lava, die flüssig aus dem Krater des Vesuvs dringt" he constructs an argument that in three pages refers to lava directly six times and by implication on several further occasions. Stifter uses the word "Lava" just once, in the context of hearsay about the Major's activities rather than as a direct statement (Uf, 187; Sf, 169).

The only basis on which we can pronounce on Stifter's use of leitmotifs is laboriously compiled lists showing the frequency and context of their occurrence. Considerations of space and the reader's patience must restrict our attention to typical examples, of which "das Ziel" may be taken first. It occurs eight times in the *Studienfassung*, only four times in the *Urfassung*. All occurrences come well before the end of the second chapter, and after the word's first appearance are linked with increasing firmness to the narrator and his relationship with the Major, rather than to the latter alone. In the third paragraph of the story the narrator refers to the Major's invitation to visit him in his "Heimat, in welcher er nunmehr ein Ziel gefunden habe" (p. 166); the narrator decides to accept, "da ich neugierig war, sein Ziel kennen zu lernen" (ibid.). Three paragraphs later the Major is referred to, despite his fifty years, as "das Ziel von manchen schönen Augen" (p. 167). After months of wandering, the narrator decides that the time has come "dem Pilgern ein Ziel zu setzen" (p. 171) and to proceed directly to the Major's estate. When the narrator and his guide have ridden some way, the former sees in the moonlight the outline of the gallows, "das Ziel meiner Begleitung" (p. 175). When the word next occurs, it has its original and precise connotation: the narrator determines at the first opportunity "den Major um das Ziel zu fragen, von dem er mir geschrieben hatte . . ." (p. 183). A few pages later we read: "Ich fragte an dem Abende dieses Tages meinen Reisefreund nicht um sein Ziel, wie ich mir tags vorher beim Schlafengehen so fest vorgenommen hatte" (p. 188). The final appearance occurs shortly after: "Ich fragte den Mann nun gar nicht mehr um sein Ziel, dessen er in seinem Briefe an mich erwähnt hatte" (p. 190). Of these eight appearances, the fourth and the last three are not found in the *Urfassung*, where there are neither other appearances of the word, nor synonyms in related contexts.

These facts justify the suggestions that Stifter was consciously developing the significance of this word (in the *Urfassung* there is no return to the original precise meaning), and that the third, fourth and fifth instances lack almost entirely the special connotation of the first and last appearances. The reason why the word does not occur at all in the second half of the story is surely that the narrator has learnt that sensitive observation and imitation of an admired exemplar is preferable to questioning him about his purpose in life.

We can now turn our attention to a word-complex that has been mentioned by most commentators of *Brigitta*: four terms that all imply desolation, barrenness, wildness. In order of their first appearance these are "öde/Öde", "Steinfeld", "Wüste/wüst", and "Wildnis/wild/Wildheit"; they occur respectively ten, four, eight and six times in the *Studienfassung*, seven, five, seven and seven times in the *Urfassung*. "Steinfeld" is used only in the literal sense of the stony ground of the Hungarian plain out of which Brigitta and the Major create their fruitful estates. "Wild" and its related words are used of Brigitta, but also of Gabriele, of the Major and his park ("eine freundliche Wildnis", p. 181), and of the "Angst und Wildheit" in Gustav's eyes when he temporarily keeps the wolves at bay (p. 219). "Öde" and "Wüste" appear more closely related.[9] "Öde" occurs in the fifth paragraph of the story, and is used three times, as adjective or noun, on that page (167), to describe the Hungarian puszta, and the desolate Vesuvian slopes on which the narrator first saw the Major; it is used again on the next page. When on page 174 "Wüste" is used, appearing three times in as many lines (and being equated with "mein altes Steinfeld"; on p. 212 we have "das öde Steinfeld"), we are tempted to see in the choice of the new word merely elegant variation. In fact Stifter is here preparing the reader for the powerful and metaphorical use of "Wüste" in the opening paragraphs of the third chapter: beauty is often overlooked "weil sie in der Wüste ist" (p. 198): the young Brigitta's isolation ("So ward die Wüste immer größer", p. 199) nevertheless has no lasting adverse effect on her "unverwüstlicher Kraft" (p. 215). The last appearance of "wüst" reveals the one striking difference in usage between the versions in this entire word-complex. The final version has the Major settle at "dem wüsten Sitze Uwar, wo er nie gewesen war" (Sf, 225); the *Urfassung* boldly applied the adjective to the man: "Wüste war er nach Uwar gegangen . . ." (Uf, 227; in this version he had been born there).

A recurrent feature of Stifter's writing is his desire to maintain a state of balance between positive and negative characteristics; this is probably the way in which he most consistently and effectively maintains tension. Even on first acquaintance with the story, most readers probably realize long before Brigitta's cry of "Stephan" (p. 222) that the Major was indeed her errant husband;[10] renewed readings reveal the extent to which tension is created by mystery, rumour and small and often unexplained details, which present sufficiently challenging problems to offset the inevitable loss of tension once the principal mystery has been revealed. What is often seen as a virtually paradisiac ending to the book in fact obscures an element that Stifter was at pains to keep neutral: the joyous reunion of long-separated husband and wife should not conceal the difficulties that lie ahead for the other two main characters. The narrator, we know, has by the time he comes to write the story overcome his youthful excesses and become integrated into society. Gustav, on the other hand, has the limitless potential of his country, but when we last see him he is still some way from a state of perfection. Critics like Gerda von Petrikovits[11] who consider him a pale, uninteresting figure, have not thought out the implications of the more negative aspects of the boy's character. Though modest, graceful, full of enthusiasm, he also displays a characteristic that was in large measure responsible for his parents' separation: passion. The word "Leidenschaft" does not occur until nearly half way through the story, but thereafter it is used seven times. Nature is "leidenschaftslos" (p. 190); on page 196 "Leidenschaft" is twice mentioned in Gömör's reported comments as the link that binds the Major to Brigitta; the narrator comments that the Major's warm praise of Brigitta on their homeward ride was spoken "ohne alle Leidenschaft" (p. 216), and shortly after he repeats, "Von einer unheimlichen Leidenschaft . . . war keine Spur" (p. 217); the narrator pities himself after witnessing the reunion of Brigitta and Stephan because his heart has known nothing but "der trüben Lohe der Leidenschaft" (p. 224); and finally, we read of Gustav's joy at discovering his father: "Am freudigsten war schier Gustav, der immer so an dem Major gehangen war, der ihn immer leidenschaftlich und einseitig den herrlichsten Mann dieser Erde nannte, und der ihn nun als Vater verehren durfte, ihn, an dem sein Auge, wie an einer Gottheit[12] hing" (p. 225). We need not doubt, now that Gustav is revealed as the binding link in a true family unit, that his future will be happy and beneficent; but the passion and one-sidedness of his praise and veneration of his father is potentially dangerous.

There are further sources of danger present in the story, counteracting its otherwise excessively idyllic optimism: the threefold mention of the baneful effects of exposure to the cold night air on the puszta, and the wolves (twice explicit, once implicit) are obvious external dangers. Dangers that come from within include Brigitta's pride, Stephan's flighty immaturity and the young couple's introverted isolation (the paragraph "Von nun an lebten sie in ihrer Wohnung fort . . .", p. 208, is particularly important in this respect, looking forward to the way in which in *Prokopus* the couple's marriage in the mountain-top castle very soon turns out to be a marriage on the rocks). There is, however, no clearcut dividing-line between "good" and "bad", as can be demonstrated by numerous details. Brigitta's demand for a love "ohne Maß und Ende" (p. 205), and the adjective that describes their embrace at the moment of reunion (her arms enfolded him "mit maßloser

Heftigkeit", p. 222),[13] indicate how narrow the divide is between happiness and grief.

A whole complex of equivocal considerations concerns Brigitta's masculinity (and to a less marked extent Stephan's "sanfte Hoheit . . ., so einfach und so siegend, daß er mehr als einmal auch Männer betörte", p. 167). The narrator's first sight of Brigitta, a rider silhouetted against the glow of the evening sun, leads him to assume that he is looking at a man. "Dieser aber war nichts anderes, als ein Weib, etwa vierzig Jahre alt, welches sonderbar genug die weiten landesmäßigen Beinkleider an hatte, und auch wie ein Mann zu Pferde saß" (p. 172). Later, when the narrator repeats comments he had heard from Gömör and others, we are told twice in three lines that Brigitta does things "wie ein Mann" (p. 196—less than two pages after the Major has referred to her as "das herrlichste Weib auf dieser Erde"). In "Steppenvergangenheit" we learn how, as a baby starved of maternal love, Brigitta began to exhibit masculine tendencies ("verdrehte sie oft die großen wilden Augen, wie Knaben tun"; "in ihrem Körper war fast Manneskraft"; "sie ritt gut und kühn, wie ein Mann"—pp. 199-200). Only as a tiny indication of her interest in Stephan Murai do we learn, when she undresses, that she had adorned herself with jewellery for the social gathering (p. 204). Then, after the breakdown of her marriage, "sie nahm Männerkleider" (p. 212)—and, as we know, has worn man's clothing since. It is as a special concession that, on the day of the narrator's first "official" visit to Maroshely, and because she was expecting the Major, she was "in Frauenkleidern und hatte ihre Geschäfte bei Seite gesetzt, weil sie den Tag für uns widmete" (p. 215).

Although the causes of Brigitta's masculine characteristics impute no blame on her, she does maintain them. In *Abdias*, written in the previous year, I discern transvestism and hubristic identification with others as an important element in the Jew's guilt. As a child he was sometimes dressed as a girl, and shown his reflection in the looking-glass (*Studien*, [II], ed. M. Stefl, 11); his beauty is compared with that of the heavenly messengers of old, his isolation in the desert with that of Mohammed (p. 12); he travels "als bewaffneter Türke" (p. 15), "gleichsam wie ein König der Karawanen" (p. 18); in the desert battle he appears "wie ein Feldherr, der da ordnet" and after it is referred to as "dem tapfern Emir"; megalomania then takes possession of his fantasies and he sees himself as Bey, Sultan, ruler of the world (p. 20). Finally, there is the carefully stage-managed departure (Uram has been sent off on a wild sheep chase) from the old desert town: an old man leading a donkey, on which sits a woman holding in her arms a baby (Stifter's choice of "das Kind" for references to Ditha at this point—p. 53—helps obscure the obvious discrepancy that in the other desert journey, the child was a boy). Although the traditional depiction of the Holy Family on its flight is artistic rather than strictly biblical, I do not think it fanciful to detect in this series of incidents (which could easily be extended) clear evidence that Abdias' labile sense of identity and position bears at least part of the responsibility for his and his family's fate. Brigitta has a clear sense of identity and position; but as long as she maintains her masculine outlook, her marriage cannot be meaningfully reconstituted.

Finally, I would like to examine some of the unequivocally positive recurrent motifs which, though they to some extent overlap and interact, may be grouped together under such categories as historical progress; mutual protection; meaningful activity and productivity; and education. Hungary's future is being hammered out (p. 171; cf. p. 166). There is youthfulness and infinite promise in both landscape ("so viel Anfang und Ursprünglichkeit", Sf, 170; "so viel Anfang und Jungfräulichkeit", Uf, 188) and, despite his being nearly fifty, in the Major ("Aus seinem Innern brach oft so etwas Ursprüngliches und Anfangsmäßiges", Sf, 169; "eine solche Gewalt der Ursprünglichkeit . . . Jünglingsseele", Uf, 186); as the narrator too comes to realize, "Wie schön und ursprünglich . . . ist die Bestimmung des Landmannes" (p. 190). The political aspects of Hungary's past, present and future are touched upon when the narrator assumes that the statues on the staircase in the Major's house are Hungarian kings, and examines the room in which he is accommodated—more like a council-chamber than a living-room (Sf, 177-8; the *Urfassung* is here briefer and also more explicit: "ein wild nationaler Geist wehte durch sie" [the rooms], Uf, 194). The country's future lies in the exploitation of its rivers and rich natural resources, as the Major explains (p. 189), and also in the planning of its political future (the forthcoming "Landtag" is mentioned in the fourth paragraph of "Steppengegenwart", p. 214).

The theme of mutual protection is expressed by two word-groups: "Bunda/Bund/Band"; and "Sitzung/Versammlung/Verein". The bunda, a garment of sewn and often decorated skins, worn with the smooth side in, and also used as a bed-cover, has clear symbolic implications from its threefold first appearance, two literal applications as it were enfolding a metaphorical extension to the estate spread out in the darkness (p. 178); the word is used again when the Major declines to give an explanation in answer to Brigitta's criticism that he had been out at night without warm clothing: he had lent his bunda to Gustav (p. 216). "Bund" is used both in a public sense ("Man hatte . . . einen Bund geschlossen, p. 194) and in a private sense (the "schöneren natürlicheren Bunde" of marriage, p. 225).

Meetings are usually referred to by "Sitzung" (Sf. 177, 178, 194; the *Urfassung* prefers "Versammlung" on the second occasion, Uf, 194), the landowners' confederation is a "Verein" (p. 212). In view of the special significance of "Versammlung", it is perhaps surprising that Stifter should also have used it for the parties given by Brigitta's father (Sf, 201, twice in one paragraph; the Urfassung has the more neutral and surely preferable "Gesellschaft", Uf, 207).

The theme of cultivation and productivity is introduced when the narrator walks at the strange horsewoman's side through her estate, noticing the contrast between it and the "Steinfeld" outside, and which "heiß und trocken herein sah zu dieser kühlen grünen Frische" (p. 173).[14] The next day the narrator begins to become acquainted with the Major's estate, his people, ideals, way of life. The Major's speech which begins: " 'Ich glaube,' sagte er einmal, 'daß man es so mit dem Boden eines Landes beginnen müsse . . .' " (p. 189) is his creed. We see later that it is closely connected with his former hopes of artistic or academic achievement (p. 191), an idea first hinted at in the reference to "das Glühendste und Dichterischste" (p. 169) of the Major's soul. Artistic achievement is in fact more Brigitta's accomplishment than the Major's: she has conjured a "Fabel" (p. 174) out of the waste land;[15] her soul "griff immer weiter um sich, der Himmel des Erschaffens senkte sich in sie . . . und in das öde Steinfeld war ein kraftvoll weiterschreitend Heldenlied gedichtet. Und die Dichtung trug, wie sie tut, auch ihren Segen" (p. 212). The image of the epic occurs in a similar context in the third chapter, "Reisebuch", of the rather later *Zwei Schwestern*: ". . . als legte die Natur ein einfach erhabenes Heldengedicht vor mich hin" (*Studien*, ed. cit., [II], 462).

Education is the last and most important of these recurrent themes. All the principal characters of *Brigitta* bear out this observation in differing ways. There is no verbal leitmotif (though the verb "lernen" occurs frequently), and much of the evidence has already appeared in other contexts. Stephan Murai, Brigitta and Gabriele are not helped by their early upbringing: Stephan's father "hatte ihn auf dem Lande auferzogen, um ihn für das Leben vorzubereiten. Als seine Erziehung vollendet war, mußte er zuerst Reisen machen, und dann sollte er die gewählte Gesellschaft seines Vaterlandes kennen lernen" (p. 201); Gabriele, the outwardly beautiful catalyst, is "ein wildes Geschöpf, das ihr Vater auf dem Lande erzog, wo er ihr alle und jede Freiheit ließ, weil er meinte, daß sie sich nur so am naturgemäßesten entfalte, und nicht zu einer Puppe gerate . . ." (p. 209); Brigitta's upbringing had been starved of love and understanding. Her son is shown abundant love, but we learn little about his education beyond the fact that he went everywhere with his mother, whose "tätige, schaffende, heischende Seele . . . floß allgemach in ihn" (p. 212). It is the education of life that helps bring Brigitta and the Major to perfection, will assuredly do the same for Gustav—and that is denied Gabriele. The narrator himself abundantly justifies the Major's trust by maturing to become a creative, integrated member of society; the older man had, as he said, learnt "Tätigkeit und Wirken" (p. 213) from Brigitta, and the narrator, as "ein Teil jenes einträchtigen Wirkens" on the estate, learnt "die Süssigkeit des Schaffens" (p. 217), and also the value of family life.

Considerations of space must exclude study of other leitmotifs—the numerous references to flowers, literal and metaphorical (the white lilies on

Gabriele's tomb, three in number in the *Urfassung*, p. 227, two in the *Studien-fassung*, p. 226, are less puzzling than Walter Haussmann[16] and Franz Mautner[17] imply if the reference in the *Urfassung* to the "Lilienstabe" of Gabriele's beauty (p. 213) is taken into consideration); the role of rumour in the story, helping preserve tension; and a whole series of related concepts that, literally from beginning to end, strengthen the sense of mystery with their reference to imprecise, veiled, smoky, cloudy and melancholic qualities in man and nature. This idea is introduced in the first sentence of the story ("Dinge und Beziehungen . . ., die uns nicht sogleich klar sind", p. 165) and is still present, transmuted but not fully resolved, in the final lines: "Mit trüben, sanften Gedanken zog ich weiter, bis die Leitha überschritten war, und die lieblichen blauen Berge des Vaterlandes vor meinen Augen dämmerten" (p. 226).

PETER BRANSCOMBE

St Andrews

NOTES

[1] Published in the *Wiener Zeitschrift für Kunst, Literatur, Theater und Mode*, 16 December 1843, pp. 1996-7, and quoted by M. Enzinger in "Stifters Erzählung 'Brigitta' und Ungarn", *Gesammelte Aufsätze zu Adalbert Stifter* (Vienna, 1967), p. 153.

[2] Page-references in the text of this article are, unless otherwise indicated, to the *Studienfassung* (abbreviated Sf where there is a possibility of ambiguity), in *Adalbert Stifter: Studien* [Vol. II], ed. Max Stefl (Augsburg, 1956), in which *Brigitta* is on pp. 165-226.

[3] Page-references to the *Urfassung* (abbreviated Uf) are to *Adalbert Stifter: Erzählungen in der Urfassung* [Vol. II], ed. M. Stefl (Augsburg, 1952), in which *Brigitta* is on pp. 181-227.

[4] E. Feise, *Xenion: Themes, Forms, and Ideas in German Literature* (Baltimore, 1950); the chapter in question is entitled "Kellers *Romeo und Julia* und Stifters *Brigitta*. Aufbau und Gestalt", pp. 165-79.

[5] Ibid., p. 167.

[6] Ibid., p. 171.

[7] In the *Studienfassung* "Schicksal" is mentioned on pp. 206, 209, 218 (twice), "Schicksalen" on p. 169, "Geschick" on pp. 207 and 225; in the *Urfassung* "Schicksal" occurs at least nine times, with "Verhängnis" and "Notwendigkeit" as synonyms in the pages describing the turning-point of the Brigitta/Stephan Murai relationship (Uf, 211-3), where there are seven reverences to Fate.

[8] K. Steffen, *Adalbert Stifter: Deutungen* (Basle and Stuttgart, 1955), here pp. 105-8.

[9] Eleonore Frey, "Dinge und Beziehungen: Zu Stifters Brigitta", *Orbis Litterarum* XXIV (1969), 52-71 fails to justify her suggestion that "Die Begriffe 'Wüste' and 'Oede' stehen für eine Masslosigkeit, die zugleich für eine Landschaft und für eine bestimmte Seelenlage Brigittas bezeichnend ist" (p. 61).

[10] F. H. Mautner exaggerates the extent of the suspense Stifter creates in the story in his lively "Randbemerkungen zu 'Brigitta' ", *Adalbert Stifter: Studien und Interpretationen* (Heidelberg, 1968), p. 89.

[11] G. von Petrikovits, "Zur Entstehung der Novelle 'Brigitta' ", *VASILO* XIV (1965), 93-104, here p. 104.

[12] In Stifter's pagan, curiously unreligious society, words that have religious connotations often appear as danger-signs, e.g. "vergöttert" (p. 198); "wie einen Engel des Lichtes verehrte er sie" (p. 205); "mit einer Verehrung, die wie an die Hinneigung zu einem höheren Wesen erinnerte . . ." (p. 218).

[13] The *Urfassung,* still more powerful and violent, made the link even stronger with the addition: "Und wie in ungemessnem Stolze führte er seine Braut herum vor allen Augen . . ." (Uf, 212).

[14] Brigitta, we learn later, stared at her father after he had chastized her, "mit den heißen trockenen Augen" (p. 200); and after Stephan had expressed his hatred of Brigitta, she looked at him "mit den trockenen, entzündeten Augen" from which, a few lines later, "heiße Tropfen" ran (p. 211).

[15] Her artistic activity was prefaced in childhood by the scraps of paper "auf denen seltsame wilde Dinge gezeichnet waren" (p. 200), and by her emotional involvement in the children's picture of fraternal sacrifice (p. 204); cf. paragraph 2 above, Stifter's entry in Emilie von Schlechta's album on 8 March 1847 (*Adalbert Stifters Leben und Werk in Briefen und Dokumenten,* Frankfurt, 1962, p. 179), and the "Vorrede" to *Bunte Steine.*

[16] W. Haussmann, "Adalbert Stifters 'Brigitta' ", *Der Deutschunterricht* III (Stuttgart, 1951), Heft 2, 30-48, here p. 46.

[17] "Randbemerkungen zu 'Brigitta' " (see footnote 10 above), pp. 101-2.

VI

FERDINAND KÜRNBERGER, FRIEDRICH SCHLÖGL AND THE FEUILLETON IN *GRÜNDERZEIT* VIENNA

When, in his essay *Hofmannsthal und seine Zeit*, Hermann Broch analyses the cultural scene in Vienna round 1880, he reaches the drastic conclusion: "An literarischer Produktion war ausser einem gefälligen Feuilletonismus so viel wie nichts vorhanden. . . ."[1] Damning as this pronouncement may be with regard to Austrian literature during the *Gründerzeit*, it also dismisses the feuilleton rather too lightly. In fact this genre not only attracted a wide range of talented writers but also produced in many cases a fascinatingly distinctive style of writing. Moreover, the feuilleton was closely integrated into Vienna's cultural life and, indeed, its social and political life, inasmuch as the latter existed at all.

The rise of the feuilleton was a consequence of the rise of Vienna's mass-circulation press, and it shared both the strengths and weaknesses of this institution. It is well known that Vienna's press was not a model of integrity: apart from Karl Kraus's attacks the English journalist Henry Wickham Steed has left a penetrating analysis of it which is also a stinging indictment.[2] The shaky foundations of Vienna's press resulted from the unfavourable conditions in which it developed: neither the persistent government interference, both direct and indirect, nor the connections with various speculators and pressure groups encouraged honesty and independence. Nevertheless, in the *Gründerzeit* the newspaper triumphed at the expense of all other forms of reading matter. In 1881 Friedrich Schlögl (1821-1892), who was both a practising journalist and an avid reader, made the following observations:

> Die Klage, dass noch zu keiner Zeit so wenig gelesen wurde, als seit den letzten zwanzig und dreissig Jahren, ist eine stereotype und gerechtfertigte, insoferne sie von buchhändlerischer Seite ergeht und sich auf das Lesen von Büchern und überhaupt tiefern Studiums und ernsterer Qualität bezieht. Trotzdem wurde nie so viel gelesen, als eben seit den geschmähten zwanzig und dreissig Jahren und ist das Lesebedürfniss ein intensives und allgemeines geworden, aber—man liest eben nur mehr Zeitungen und was in die Rubrik dieser typischen Eintagsfliegen rangirt. . . . Nur der minimalste Bruchteil beschäftigt sich noch mit der Lectüre von Büchern, ansonst genügt der Menge die "Zeitung".[3] (*Werke*, III, 162-3)

This passage occurs in a feuilleton entitled "Beim Tabakkrämer", a circumstance which merits a brief explanation. In late nineteenth-century Vienna (as today) the small tobacconist's was the chief outlet for newspapers and journals intended for the mass of readers, and his shop was, as Schlögl indicates, a centre of social life and local gossip. The tobacconist was often also an agent for the state lottery, an institution which the Viennese had surrounded with a web of ritual and lore. Both lottery and tobacco were state monopolies, and the tobacconist was often a war veteran or his widow who had been granted a concession. The state could and did keep a watchful eye on what was sold. One of the most effective measures the authorities could take against a newspaper which they found offensive was to ban the sale of individual copies, thus depriving it of that very outlet which was so well integrated into the lives of so many Viennese from such a wide social background.

Inevitably the rise of the newspaper and the attendant developments in reading habits and readership influenced writers and what they wrote. A prose writer could reach his widest audience through the columns of a newspaper; indeed, he could make his name solely by publishing in this medium —this was the case with Schlögl, as he himself acknowledged.[4] There was considerable demand: a popular daily such as the *Illustriertes Wiener Extrablatt* published novels and thrillers in serial form. But, apart from such material designed to ensure that readers purchased a newspaper regularly, there was—by the eighteen-seventies—an established tradition of short prose forms: in the early years of the nineteenth century Joseph Schreyvogel's *Sonntagsblatt* had already set high standards in this field. Indeed, as a result of this tradition there was a tendency in the newspapers of Vienna's *Gründerzeit* to devote a fair amount of space to the topical but not too specific essay, often introducing specifically Viennese material and often aspiring to a more literary style beyond the immediate demands of journalism. It is impossible to give a detailed definition of the Viennese feuilleton: the range of material covered by the articles under this heading was extremely wide, and the basic unifying feature was merely the manner of publication. The feuilleton generally appeared at the bottom of the first page of a newspaper; it was thus an indispensable part of a newspaper, and at the same time incidental by nature, appearing, as the Viennese said "unter dem Strich", under the line which ruled off the part of the page devoted to news and leaders. Its place of publication gave it the air of a commentary or footnote, as well as implying that the feuilleton was to be a rather light-hearted and entertaining contrast to the serious news. If the newspaper became, as Schlögl suggested, the staple "Leseproviant", then the feuilletons were "leicht verdaulich", as Daniel Spitzer, another very popular Feuilletonist of the *Gründerzeit*, described his own weekly offerings, which he called *Wiener Spaziergänge*.[5]

As Schlögl's and Spitzer's choice of culinary imagery might indeed suggest, the feuilleton soon became an institution, an accepted part of Vienna's cultural life in the last decades of the Habsburg Empire. The *Neue Freie Presse* enjoyed the most prestige, in this as in other respects; if a young author's writings were accepted for publication in its feuilleton, then he had achieved recognition. It was here that the essays of the young Hofmannsthal appeared; and in *Die Welt von Gestern* (1941) Stefan Zweig tells of his own youthful pride at having an essay accepted for publication there and of the respect and standing he consequently enjoyed. More generally, he states that what appeared in the feuilleton of the *Neue Freie Presse* invariably provided a talking-point for the educated bourgeoisie of Vienna, and was regarded by those without any deep interest in cultural matters as an authoritative pronouncement.[6] Spitzer's Sunday feuilletons were for decades an indispensable talking-point; as a contemporary commentator put it, "Ein Mensch, der Sonntags um 12 Uhr noch nicht das Feuilleton des "Wiener Spaziergängers" gelesen und darüber in Entzücken gerathen wäre, würde es nicht wagen, sich in einer anständigen Gesellschaft zu zeigen."[7] Such a lively interest in the feuilleton was not, however, confined to a narrow social range; Schlögl's tobacconist turned newsagent also expresses firm views on the worth of various feuilleton writers to his customers. The individual "Feuilletonisten" become well-known personalities, a popular and characteristic part of Viennese life. What and how they wrote gives a valuable guide to and commentary on the interests and attitudes of their fellow citizens.

The feuilleton was both product and reflection of Viennese circumstances and attitudes. It was both a form of entertainment and a form of expression which Vienna's best writers were happy to use. Moreover, this mixture of unserious form and often serious content appealed to the Viennese taste for indirect and intricate modes of expression, itself to a large extent a result of those decades of censorship which had taught the Viennese to look for serious comments in unlikely places. Such attitudes persisted among both readers and writers long after restrictions had been eased: hence we find among the feuilletons of the later nineteenth-century some of the most penetrating and blunt criticisms of Vienna and the Viennese.

Ferdinand Kürnberger (1823-1879) is the outstanding writer in this respect. Hermann Bahr, in his bitter essay *Wien* (1906)—a work which demonstrates well the characteristic love-hate relationship of Viennese writers to their city—writes of him:

> Und das ist auch wienerisch, dass er, der mit seiner Einsicht in jedes Problem, mit seinem Trieb zum Notwendigen, mit seinem Gefühl für die Forderungen der Zeit, mit seinem Mut, mit seiner Kraft überall sonst ein Mann der Tat geworden wäre, hier ins Feuilleton gesteckt wurde. Man liess in Gottes Namen einmal die Wahrheit zu, doch nur unter dem Strich. . . . Man verzieh ihm, dass er ein Mann war, weil er den Narren gab, den Feuilletonisten, der ja doch nur spasst. (*Wien*, p. 107)

Although Kürnberger also wrote dramas, Novellen and novels, among which the novel *Der Amerikamüde* (1855) was deservedly successful, his most powerful and masterly writing is to be found in his feuilletons, the most important of which were republished during his lifetime in two collections: *Siegelringe* (1874) and *Literarische Herzenssachen* (1877).[8] These are quoted extensively by Bahr in his *Wien* essay, an entire chapter of which is devoted to Kürnberger. Wickham Steed also thought highly of Kürnberger's analyses of Vienna and the Viennese: to judge from the material quoted in *The Hapsburg Monarchy* (introduction and pp. 202-6) he got to know of Kürnberger through Bahr's essay, and calls him "the ablest Austrian essayist of the second half of the nineteenth century" (ibid., p. xv). Karl Kraus was also interested in Kürnberger, which is not surprising, as Kürnberger was in many ways his spiritual forbear, attacking both the linguistic usage of the Viennese press (for example, in "Sprache und Zeitungen" [1866] and "Die Blumen des Zeitungstils" [1872/6], *Werke*, II, 8-32) and its lack of integrity and honesty.[9]

The scope of Friedrich Schlögl's writings is far more restricted: whereas Kürnberger tries to probe the foundations of Viennese existence, Schlögl is content to present its surface in the greatest detail. In this respect Schlögl represents the culmination of a tradition of short prose forms describing aspects of Viennese life which has its roots in the pamphlet literature of the reign of Joseph II, but he was also a revered master for the many writers who produced countless examples of the same genre, generally known as the "Wiener Skizze", for the feuilleton columns of Vienna's newspapers in the late nineteenth and early twentieth centuries. It is as "der klassische Meister der Wiener Skizze" that Schlögl occasionally finds his way into histories of literature; despite this, his chief claim to fame nowadays is probably that he coined the phrase "Wiener Blut" as the title for the first and most successful collection of his feuilletons. It was published in 1873, and within three years had not only been reprinted three times but had also provided Johann Strauss with the title for his waltz, op. 354; the title was of course also used for an operetta, the music of which was put together by Adolf Müller the Younger from Strauss's compositions.

Both Kürnberger and Schlögl were born in Vienna and grew up there.[10] Their families were poor, but followed traditional occupations well known from Viennese local literature: Kürnberger's father, for instance, was a lamplighter, and his mother kept a stall on the Naschmarkt. Both Kürnberger and Schlögl, like so many of Vienna's young talents in the first half of the nineteenth century, attended the prestigious Schottengymnasium, although Schlögl was forced to leave prematurely in order to make his contribution to the family income. Throughout his life Kürnberger derived a meagre existence from his work as a free-lance journalist and writer, never holding any more permanent position than a part-time post as secretary of the Schiller-Stiftung from 1866 to 1870. Schlögl entered the bureaucracy at the very bottom of the ladder and, after years of drudgery and snail-like promotion, eventually retired on health grounds in 1870: it was only then that he was able to become a full-time man of letters.

Both men were in their late twenties when the stormy events of March 1848 broke out in Vienna. Both reacted with considerable enthusiasm and played an active part. For Kürnberger the revolution brought the first opportunity to practise journalism extensively. Schlögl was the author of some verses entitled "An Einen" which appeared in the *Theaterzeitung* on 25 March 1848; these were a thinly disguised appeal to Grillparzer to express publicly his reaction to the revolution. Schlögl also led a deputation which sought better working conditions for the lowly grade of civil servants to which he belonged. Although by the end of the year Kürnberger had been forced into uncomfortable nomadic exile and Schlögl had returned to the anonymity of his bureaucrat's desk, the revolutionary spring of 1848 left an indelible mark on the characters of both writers. More than thirty years later, in a lecture given on 28 January 1882, Schlögl expressed the desire to be remembered as "ein echtfärbiger 48er".[11] The experiences of the revolution and the reaction which followed it left in both Schlögl and Kürnberger a mixture of idealism and cynicism; they were inspired by the potential power of a popular political movement, yet disheartened by the rapidity with which the spirit of 1848 degenerated and crumbled, and, especially, by the behaviour of so many Viennese who, after the revolution had collapsed, not only abandoned all thoughts of loyalty to save their own skins, but also were more than eager to denounce their fellow citizens. The behaviour of the Viennese in 1848 and 1849 explains in part the love-hate attitude towards them shown by both Kürnberger and Schlögl. They had shown what they were and what they could be, and when, in the 1860s, political comment was again possible, both writers never tired of castigating the middle classes of Vienna for their lack of interest and participation in political affairs, nor of applauding even the slightest piece of evidence that the old attitudes were changing.

Kürnberger and Schlögl remained disillusioned revolutionaries through-out their lives, and cynicism and a sense of frustration underlie much of their writing. They are both extremely pessimistic about the chances of Viennese society taking a turn for the better, and indeed are resigned to this state of affairs. They take a gloomy view, and are seldom disappointed: several of Kürnberger's feuilletons begin with phrases like "Dacht' ich es doch . . .". The "Skizze" with which Schlögl chose to end his collection *Wienerisches* (1882) is devoted to the figure of Herr von Grammerstädter, a dyed-in-the-wool Viennese *Spiessbürger* from the property-owning middle classes of the inner suburbs; the feuilleton and thus also the book end with the phrase: "Alles Hoffen vergebens, das Grammerstädterthum wird siegen." (*Werke*, III, 376) Alongside such pessimism both writers display a deeply emotional reaction to Vienna. But these emotions do not mean unconditional acceptance. Especially for Kürnberger, the city is the ungrateful beloved, and it is only grudgingly that he will admit the fascination it has for him. At the beginning of "Ein Besuch in Wien" (1865) he writes: "Von Zeit zu Zeit seh' ich die Alte gern." But a few sentences later he adds: "Ich, der ihre Geschichte im Herzen trage wie wenige ihrer Söhne". (*Werke*, I, 478-9)

It is this complex emotional attachment to Vienna and its *genius loci* which to a large extent compromises the satirical vein which naturally results from the negative attitude Kürnberger and Schlögl adopt towards so many aspects of Viennese life. Moreover, as the phrases just quoted show, this emotional attachment is quite obvious in their writings, even where some aspect of Viennese life is being rationally rejected and attacked. The feuilleton form does not help here, since it encourages the writer to give a highly personal view. In their feuilletons Kürnberger and Schlögl speak directly to the reader, often beginning, linking and ending them in the first person, as well as narrating in them personal experiences; there is no intermediary, no fictitious narrator to give an ironic distancing and present a detached perception of the absurd. But equally the feuilleton encourages many techniques which are decidedly satirical and which Kürnberger and Schlögl repeatedly exploit. Indeed their feuilletons, especially when collected in book form, remind the reader that a basic quality of satire is its diversity of material, that it is filled with many things, and that, as A. B. Kernan has suggested, its plot is "roughly that of a newsreel".[12] And among their favourite stylistic devices we find quotation, parody, paraphrase, invective, the juxtaposition and confusion of the material and the spiritual, of the ridiculous and the sublime, cacophony, the use of proper names and lists of inordinate length: in other words the full arsenal of the satirist.

Gründerzeit Vienna undoubtedly offered the would-be satirist a wealth of material. The city was undergoing a period of rapid expansion and change. Its outward appearance was being transformed by the demolition of the walls surrounding the inner city; the area they had occupied, together with the surrounding glacis, was being covered by the magnificent boulevard of the Ringstrasse and a series of monumental public buildings and luxury apartment blocks in a medley of historical styles. Later, around the turn of the century, when further historic areas were demolished and rebuilt in a process that was euphemistically known as "Regulierung", many writers used the feuilleton as a vehicle for protest and for the popularization of conservationist ideas. Strangely enough, such an approach does not seem to have occurred to Kürnberger and Schlögl, despite the fact that Kürnberger especially played an important role in the successful campaign to prevent the deforestation of the Wienerwald. Instead, the two writers stress the destructive aspect of the rebuilding and see in the fabric of the new Vienna a manifestation of the false values which they consider to be invading its social, cultural, political and economic life. They see everywhere the erosion of older genuine values and the triumph of pretence. The new buildings represent not wealth but debts. Fortunes are made not by hard work but by gambling—either at the roulette table or the stock exchange. The Austrian state itself is merely being driven even deeper into debt by the rapid economic expansion. If their attitudes in this sphere show Kürnberger and Schlögl to be as conservative as most other satirists, their uneasiness seems to have been well-founded in view of the crash of 1873 and the spate of accusations and trials which followed it. Despite the underlying similarity of their perceptions, the two writers chose to focus on different subjects and perspectives. But the close spiritual kinship is clear throughout their writings on Vienna and the Viennese, and it is not surprising that the two men got on well with each other at a personal level, although Kürnberger especially was generally a gruff eccentric to the rest of the world.[13]

Kürnberger tries to present the patterns which he sees underlying contemporary Viennese life. As a feuilletonist he takes some matter of current interest as his starting point—it may be some political or cultural event or controversy, it may be another article or newly published book, or it may merely be a recent personal experience—and uses it to illustrate (and more often than not attack) some aspect of Austrian life. In this sense the chief subject of his feuilletons is Austria and the Austrians, with Vienna and the Viennese used metonymically, perhaps because, as had been suggested as early as 1843, "ein Österreich, Österreicher, eine österreichische Nationalität gibt es nicht, und hat es nicht gegeben, wenn man eine Spanne Land um Wien herum ausnimmt."[14] This view was endorsed seventy years later by Wickham Steed, who noted that "to trace the genesis of 'Vienna' would be to write a psychological history of the Austrian Empire." (op. cit., p. 203) Like so many Austrian writers, Kürnberger seems principally concerned to define and characterize Austria. Many of his feuilletons are part of that desperate quest for national identity which for so long was such a characteristic part of Austrian existence. At the time Kürnberger wrote most of his feuilletons, that is to say in the decade or so after 1865, this problem was acutely topical: in addition to the relentless Prussian drive for hegemony in the German-speaking world the Austrians had to cope with growing nationalist aspirations in the provinces of the Empire and especially, of course, with the *Ausgleich* of 1867 and its implications. The problem was almost as difficult to present and solve in words as in terms of political action. Austria had to be presented as an antithesis to Germany; for if it was not different from Germany, why should Austria not be part of Germany? Rhetorically effective as such a presentation was, it meant defining Austria not in terms of itself but in terms of what it was not. Austria's protagonists tried to turn negatives into positives: in response to German inability to understand Austrian affairs, the *Neue Freie Presse* (*Abendblatt*, 10 November 1871, p. 1) had explained Austria as "das Land der Unwahrscheinlichkeiten, der Unbegreiflichkeiten, der Absurditäten". This prompted Kürnberger to write the tirade of his masterly feuilleton "Asiatisch und Selbstlos" (1871) (*Werke*, I, 193-9) since, as he pointed out, "Mit Un's definiert und erklärt man nicht." He states forcefully that the distinctive quality in Austrian life is "das Asiatische". Vienna he defines as "eine europäisch-asiatische Grenzstadt" and Austria as follows:

> Auf einem uralten Untergrund keltischen Leichtsinns das Alluvium slawischer und ostländischer Liederlichkeit im lebendig-flutenden

Strom, im täglich-stündlichen Grenzverkehr, im unaufhörlichen Emp-
fangen und Aufnehmen; *Voilà l'Autriche!* Das ist Oesterreich! (*Werke*,
I, 194)

The choice of words in this definition scarcely indicates approval; or to look
at the matter from a different angle, those very qualities which Kürnberger
selects as characteristically Austrian are ones of which he disapproves
strongly. The combination of definition and invective tends to undermine
the credibility of both, and suggests that the underlying antithesis, which
is developed and elaborated with considerable skill throughout this feuilleton,
has no other validity than as a rhetorical pattern. Moreover, Kürnberger
is forced to undermine his neat symmetrical structure in order to convey
his ideas: Austria and Vienna are presented both as an antithesis to Europe
(and, in particular, Germany), and as a synthesis of Europe and Asia. In
the concluding paragraphs of this feuilleton complexity nearly turns into
confusion (perhaps intentionally) as questions, hypotheses and negatives
accumulate.

The ambivalent and ambiguous patterns and attitudes of "Asiatisch und
Selbstlos" reflect and, one might say, express the difficulty which Kürnberger had in trying to come to terms with Austria's political and cultural
traditions. Like Schlögl, he was in general pro-German, and certainly the
superiority of German culture is implied throughout his writings. But he
is forced to recognize not only that Austrian culture is not the same as
German culture—that, for example, the dominant position of the German
language in Vienna does not give a guide to the city's true character—but
also that the admixture of non-German elements (which he may define as
"Asiatic", "Slav", "Celtic", or "Jewish") makes Austria what it is. The
existence and value of these elements and the national groups associated
with them must be acknowledged by Kürnberger's German-speaking com-
patriots if the Austria to which he is so attached is to survive as a political
and cultural entity. In view of such complexities it is not surprising that
Kürnberger has recourse to a complex style. Whereas the antithesis represents an attempt to impose a symmetrical rhetorical pattern, the paradox,
which Kürnberger also exploits extensively, admits that an obviously logical
and analytical presentation is impossible. In another feuilleton, "Hebbel
und Bauernfeld" (1872), (*Werke*, I, 208-214) he defines the nature of the
Austrian state by means of the phrase, "Oesterreich ist eine Monarchie,
temperiert durch Sr. Majestät allergetreueste Majestätsbeleidiger." Here
the paradox is turned into a principle and, indeed, Kürnberger frequently
turns to the paradox as the only means of characterizing Austrian affairs.
Such a principle as this, namely that Austria's most loyal citizens are in
fact those whose behaviour is least loyal, can give rise to a whole series of
paradoxes. In "Asiatisch und Selbstlos" Kürnberger looks at his proposition
from a different angle when he suggests: "Ich mache mich anheischig, in
Oesterreich die gefährlichste aller Revolutionen anzuzetteln, indem ich

meuchlings die Gesetze Oesterreichs befolge" (*Werke*, I, 197). Similarly structured formulations arise when Kürnberger turns his attention to a habit of the *Gründerzeit* of which he was particularly critical, namely the fashion of erecting monuments. This he interpreted as the attempt of the nonentities who formed and participated in the endless committees and societies for the construction of monuments to acquire fame and glory for themselves by exploiting the reputations of great men. And so, in "Ein Aphorismus zur Denkmal-Pest unserer Zeit" (1872), he produced the irony-laden sentence, "Man setzt Denkmäler, um unbekannte Grössen bekannt zu machen" (*Werke*, II, 290). The false values of Viennese society in the *Gründer-zeit* are thus expressed in terms of a clever inversion of what Kürnberger implies to be normal accepted Western European values: in Vienna, the "Capua der Geister", he says that both he and Grillparzer have perceived "dass man in Capua Baron wird, wofür man auswärts—ins Zuchthaus käme" (*Werke*, II, 272). Kürnberger's Austria is not merely a complex but also a topsyturvy world: in the light of his own evidence, his suggestion that "Austriazismus" is but a neologism for "Byzantinismus" (*Werke*, II, 293) seems almost an understatement.

To turn from Kürnberger to Schlögl is to turn from the foundations to the bricks and mortar of *Gründerzeit* Vienna. Schlögl reproduces the every-day life of suburban Vienna in the greatest detail, delighting especially in naming and classifying an enormous number of stock types by occupation, behaviour or character. Although his pseudo-scientific approach creates primarily a satirical effect, it is not surprising that he should have been invited to contribute a chapter on "Wiener Volksleben" to the volume *Wien* (1886) of *Die Österreichisch-Ungarische Monarchie in Wort und Bild*, a lavish encyclopedia initiated under the editorship of Crown Prince Rudolph. Appropriately enough, in the 1880s, Schlögl also wrote a guide-book to Vienna (*Wien* = Vols. 33 and 34 of *Städtebilder und Landschaften aus aller Welt*, Linz, n.d.). In this work Schlögl again turns to those types who had earlier formed the subject of so many of his feuilletons. Like Kürnberger, Schlögl often defines and satirizes at the same time. Although the targets of his satire are far less weighty than Kürnberger's, he shows himself to belong to the best satirical traditions by seeing the dunce as mankind's worst enemy. The theory and practice of stupidity forms the subject of a lecture given by Schlögl on 22 February 1882 and entitled "Über Dummheit".[15] Many of his examples had previously formed the basis of one of his "Skiz-zen". He also claims that the intellectual and moral worth of a people should be judged on the basis not only of their work but also of their charac-teristic forms of entertainment. He imagines that one of his *Spiessbürger* figures might say: " 'No ja! Wann m'r 'n Leuten nit amal a unschuldig's Vagnüg'n vergunnt! Lachen wird der Mensch do no därfen?' ", to which he himself adds: "Gewiss, die Hauptsache ist nur: über was?" And so, appro-priately enough among the Viennese, whom Schiller had first branded as "das Volk der Fajaken",[16] it is the pursuit of pleasure on which Schlögl most frequently casts his satirical eye. It is not that he is opposed to *Gemüt-lichkeit* as such, but rather that he wishes this quintessentially Viennese quality and the traditional values connected with it not to be lost in the transformation of Vienna into a modern city.

A technique which Schlögl and his fellow "Lokalfeuilletonisten" found to be well suited to this brand of satire was the introduction of named characters to represent a certain type of Viennese. Schlögl's most famous creation was Herr von Grammerstädter—the particle indicating of course his social standing with those around him and not a patent of nobility. He is described (and in the guide-book *Wien* also pictured, along with some other well-known types: ibid., pp. 164-5 and 168-9) as an "emeritirter Fabrikant und mehrfacher vielstöckiger Eckhausherr' who lives off his accumulated wealth. He has no interest in politics, since his conviction is "Mir können's eh nit ändern". He is in fact merely a rather wealthier and more sedate version of a type not invented by Schlögl, but known to him and Viennese dialect as "Biz". In "Biz Vater und Comp." (*Werke*, III, 31-38), where the title characteristically transfers the language of business to the sphere of entertainment, since Biz's company consists of his boon companions, Schlögl sketches the existence of his type:

> In den ersten Vormittagsstunden wird die Meerschaumpfeife, welche die Tagesordnung trifft, geputzt und werden die Vögel gefüttert (zwei Verrichtungen, die er sich nicht nehmen lässt, denn "etwas zu thun" ist er gewöhnt), worauf zu einem Fabelfrühstück und einem kleinen Plausch das Stammwirthshaus (im Bezirke) besucht wird. Dort wartet nicht nur ein Cercle vertrautester Freunde auf ihn, es erwartet ihn auch sein "Stückl Spitzfleisch" mit dem "Tazerl" Essigkren, wozu drei—vier gespritzte Viertel vertilgt werden, welche Beschäftigung unter normalen Verhältnissen die Zeit bis ein Uhr Mittags ausfüllt. Dann geht's zum häuslichen Tische (selten mit Appetit), darauf ein kurzes "Schlaferl" und (längstens!) um drei Uhr ins gewohnte Café, zum gewohnten Tapper, der bis sieben Uhr währt, worauf wieder der Marsch ins Stammwirthshaus angetreten oder ein "Rutscher" vor die Linie unternommen wird.[17] (*Werke*, III, 35)

Biz's life exemplifies that "Genusssucht"—the pursuit of entertainment rather than pleasure—for which the Viennese had so often been censured. This diligently pursued quest is, however, an attempt to escape from more serious and unpleasant things: politics and political responsibility on the one hand, an unharmonious and row-ridden family life on the other. The unpalatable nature of married existence is a traditional comic theme exploited by Schlögl when he deals with middle-class characters such as Biz, Grammerstädter and his "echter Spiesser", although it is conspicuously absent from his sentimental portraits of poor families. But, then, the tendency for home life to be unpleasant and unimportant has both been influenced by and itself influenced the character of Viennese life: Schlögl gives another of his types bent on entertainment the motto "nur nit z'Haus gehn!" Nevertheless, Biz's behaviour represents an ideal and earns him considerable standing with those around him:

> Er ist geliebt (von seinen "Freundeln") weil er unerschöpflich in Erfindung von und in Ausdauer bei allen "Hetzen" ist; er ist geehrt, weil er ein unabhängiger, "aufrechter" Mann, der "sein Sacherl im Trock'nen" hat und nicht mehr zu arbeiten braucht; er ist geachtet, weil er splendid und "schenerös" ist und im Laufe der Jahre schon Hunderte von "Masseln" und Litern spendirte: er ist angestaunt seiner Leistungen bei den üblichen Zechgelagen, dann seiner Unverwüstlichkeit und ehernen Gesundheit wegen, und weil er mit einem Habitus begnadet ist, dem er unbeschadet der nöthigen Erhaltung des steten Gleichgewichts schon ein "Bünkel auffihängen" kann; und er ist schliesslich gefürchtet, weil seine Zunge und sein rechter Arm immer parat sind, Denjenigen mit einem einzigen Wort niederzudonnern und mit einem einzigen "Tupfer" niederzuschlagen, der es wagen würde, mit ihm "käwi" zu sein. (*Werke*, III, 34)

Love, honour, respect, astonishment, fear: the references to such emotions are incongruous in the trivial context, showing both the topsyturvy values of Biz and his companions and the way in which they reduce noble emotions to trivial diminutives. Schlögl satirically transfers deep and serious emotions to the sphere of superficial entertainment, thereby expressing a way of life which, in the figures of Biz and Grammerstädter, provokes in the author the whole range of negative responses from carping criticism through bitterness to despair. Despite such pessimism, Schlögl's attitude to these types is still ambivalent: he begins his first "Biz" feuilleton by noting how Biz appreciates the old style of *Volkssänger* to which he himself was deeply attached. But, then, Biz and Grammerstädter are as distinctive a part of *Gründerzeit* Vienna as Schögl himself.

The fascination which even apparently unacceptable parts of Viennese life hold for Schlögl is clear from the style of his feuilletons, of which the descriptions of Biz's way of life are typical. It is not an easy style to read, and it presupposes that the reader shares the author's total fascination with the minutiae of Viennese life. Its basic principle is that one word cannot suffice where there is the possibility of using two or more; its heavily ornamental quality might be described as "baroque". Extensive quotation and the use of dialect words and phrases produce a mosaic-like and static effect, which offers a complete contrast to Kürnberger's relentlessly dynamic prose, despite the many techniques the two writers share.

It can be seen that both Kürnberger and Schlögl are extremely sceptical about the supposed march of progress in Vienna. Kürnberger, indeed, seems resigned to the end of old Austria. "Warum stirbt Oesterreich so jammervoll schwer und langsam," we find him asking at the beginning of "Politischer Allerseelentag" (1871, *Werke*, I, 188-93), and he goes on to comment: "Seit der byzantinischen Tragödie gab's keine so musterhafte mehr wie die österreichische." Schlögl tends to cast nostalgic glances at the past: there is much of the belief in "die gute alte Zeit" in him. Although he has many harsh words for life before 1848, he is already helping to create the idyllic image of Biedermeier Vienna which has subsequently enjoyed such popularity and publicity. In their feuilletons Kürnberger and Schlögl can be seen shaping these ideas which are so characteristic of the last decades of the Habsburg Empire. Their criticisms of *Gründerzeit* Vienna do not, however, seem to have been particularly effective. Predictably it was Schlögl who enjoyed the greater popularity: Kürnberger's attacks were rather too near the mark and, not surprisingly, some of his most forceful feuilletons were first published not in Vienna but in Berlin. Moreover, the more the feuilleton became an established part of Vienna's cultural life, the less likely it was to be considered by its readers as a vehicle for ideas seriously intended to influence and change that way of life. And it was this very development of the genre into an institution and a socially accepted form of entertainment that enabled the "Feuilletonisten" to express independent critical opinions amidst all the endeavours of the government and others to shape the press to their own needs. As if to make the "Feuilletonisten" realize that their position was a special concession, the occasional feuilleton was suppressed by the authorities: Kürnberger especially soon found that there were limits to what might be said. Under such pressures the tendency of both Kürnberger and Schlögl to indulge in what is frequently little more than carping criticism is understandable; indeed, the attitude of Viennese readers encouraged it too. Ten years after Schlögl's death we find a fellow journalist referring to him as "der Oberraunzer der Stadt Wien",[18] and even a post-war critic has noted: "Kürnberger findet . . . nicht aus dem Schwarm derer heraus, die Österreich totnörgeln."[19] "Schimpfe bei jeder Sache über die Nebensache," (*Werke*, I, 211) was Kürnberger's command to those who wanted to grumble and criticize in the accepted Austrian manner; and Schlögl's feuilletons provide a perfect illustration. His heaviest strictures are directed against those who tread on his toes, sit on his coat tails, drag into everyday conversations matters he would rather not discuss or be reminded of, misuse cutlery, condiments and napkins, and so on. Broch's "gefälliger Feuilletonismus" points but to the tip of the iceberg: unlikely as it may seem at first glance, the feuilleton reveals itself as an expression in miniature of the complexities and paradoxes of Austrian society in the closing decades of the nineteenth century.

L. H. BAILEY

Vienna

NOTES

[1] Hermann Broch, *Hofmannsthal und seine Zeit: Eine Studie* (Munich, 1954), p. 51.

[2] Henry Wickham Steed, *The Hapsburg Monarchy* (London, 1913), pp. 181-201.

[3] Unless otherwise indicated, references for Schlögl's writings are to: *Gesammelte Werke*, 3 vols., Vienna/Pest/Leipzig, 1893. This comprises: I, *Wiener Blut* (1873); II, *Wiener Luft* (1875); III, *Wienerisches* (1882).

[4] See the *Geleitsbrief* to *Wiener Blut* (*Werke*, I, 17).

[5] See Schlögl: *Werke*, III, 163; Spitzer: *Wiener Spaziergänge* VII (= *Letzte Wiener Spaziergänge*, Vienna, 1894), 257.

[6] Stefan Zweig: *Die Welt von Gestern* (London/Stockholm, 1941). See pp. 81-2 and pp. 87-8 of the Fischer Bücherei edition, Frankfurt/Hamburg, 1970. For the social and cultural significance of the "Feuilletonisten" see also E. Wechsler: *Wiener Autoren* (Leipzig, 1888), especially pp. 177-187.

[7] Don Spavento (pseud.): *Wiener Schriftsteller und Journalisten* (Vienna, 1874), pp. 16-7. The passage is quoted in another useful work on the *Gründerzeit* feuilleton, E. Eckstein: *Beiträge zur Geschichte des Feuilletons*, 2 vols., Leipzig, 1876.

[8] Unless otherwise indicated, references to Kürnberger's writings are to the first two volumes of the incomplete *Werke* (ed. O. E. Deutsch), Munich/Leipzig, 1910. These are annotated and enlarged editions of: I, *Siegelringe* (1874), II, *Literarische Herzenssachen* (1877).

[9] See, for example, the following items in *Die Fackel*: "Ferdinand Kürnberger und die Wiener Presse" (No. 124, Dec. 1902, pp. 1-2); "Ferdinand Kürnberger: 'Die Geschichte meines Passes' " (No. 214-5, Dec. 1906, pp. 7-38); "Briefe Ferdinand Kürnbergers" (No. 288, Oct. 1909, pp. 4-12).

[10] The basic compilations of biographical material on the two writers are to be found in doctoral dissertations submitted to the Philosophische Fakultät of the University of Vienna. See especially: Julius Halpern: *Ferdinand Kürnberger* (1928); Anton Öllerer: *Friedrich Schlögl* (1928).

[11] Text printed as: *Aus Alt- und Neu-Wien*, Vienna, 1882. See p. 30.

[12] A. B. Kernan: *The Plot of Satire* (New Haven/London, 1965), p. 97.

[13] See, for example, the obituary by Schlögl entitled "Von Ferdinand Kürnberger, dem Menschen" in *Der Heimgarten*, Vol. IV, No. 3 (Dec. 1879), pp. 212-6. Compare the account which Peter Rosegger gives of his first meeting with Kürnberger in his *Gute Kameraden* (Leipzig, 1916), pp. 278-283.

[14] The comment appears in: Viktor von Andrian-Werburg: *Österreich und dessen Zukunft* (Hamburg, 1843), p. 8.

[15] The text was printed as the feuilleton in the *Konstitutionelle Vorstadt-Zeitung* Vol. 28, Nos. 55-6, 24 and 25 February 1882.

[16] See the *Xenion* headed "Donau in O**" in the *Musenalmanach für das Jahr 1797*. This runs:
   Mich umwohnet mit glänzendem Aug das Volk der Fajaken,
   Immer ists Sonntag, es dreht immer am Heerd sich der Spiess.
Text quoted from *Werke* (National-Ausgabe, Weimar, 1943), I, 321.

[17] The most satisfactory explanations of Schlögl's dialect expressions are to be found in F. S. Hügel: *Der Wiener Dialekt. Lexikon der Wiener Volkssprache*, Vienna/Pest/Leipzig, 1873.

[18] The phrase occurs in a passage quoted in *Die Fackel* No. 124 (Dec. 1902), p. 1.

[19] The phrase is from L. Reiter: *Österreichische Staats- und Kulturgeschichte* (Klagenfurt, 1947) and is quoted in W. Immergut: *Ferdinand Kürnberger und Österreich* (Diss., Vienna, 1952), p. 125.

VII

"DIES ÖSTERREICH IST EINE KLEINE WELT"

When considering Austrian literature, we confront a paradox: the need to insist upon its "Austrianness" and its universality at the same time. Of course, mere subject-matter need not restrict a work of art: *Moby Dick* is not simply about whaling; but geographical limitation of the highly specific kind we find in Austrian literature, and the concentration that we also find on problems apparently peculiar to a specific sort of society, suggest narrowness. To claim the problems are, in practical terms, universal, would be to oversimplify and probably misunderstand them. The key lies in the differing ways in which "local elements" can be used, and there are essentially three of these.

First, there is "Heimatliteratur", where "local colour" is evoked more or less as an end in itself. The existence of a world outside the one portrayed is ignored; where this is done deliberately, we speak of an idyll, where unwittingly, we call it "provincialism".

Second, an author chooses a setting appropriate to, and illustrative of, his theme, which can be stated separately from it. *Buddenbrooks* fits Lübeck well, but is not inextricably bound to it. Fontane's Prussia, for all his attachment to it and involvement in it (witness the *Wanderungen durch die Mark Brandenburg*), is, as he makes abundantly clear in the very first lines of *Der Stechlin*, only illustrative or symptomatic of the great changes going on in the outside world, with which it has mysterious, subterranean connections.

Third, an author may present his restricted world and assert that it is an image of the way the world is. Such an assertion, which is not drawing general conclusions from insufficient data, but performing an imaginative and artistic act, must, if it is properly recognised, disarm criticism of the local and restricted nature of its subject-matter.

We should be concerned with the perception of a pattern in what is shown to us, and not with the origin of the individual components of that pattern or their significance outside the work of art, though the pattern itself may have implications for the world outside. In discussing the problem of Austrian literature, I shall be taking examples almost exclusively from Kraus and Nestroy, in such a way as to correspond to the distinction I have adumbrated between the perception of a pattern and the conscious use of that pattern as a model for behaviour. It should be evident that the more restricted the basic material is, the more readily a pattern will emerge, and this applies equally to the pattern brought out by artistic methods and the pattern which, far from being the object of aesthetic contemplation, is falsely used to regulate the world from which it has been derived. It may be as well to clarify this final point by restatement in different terms, since it sums up a set of attitudes which are essentially Viennese and, as such, form the basis for the worlds which Kraus and Nestroy present to us. I am suggesting that the Viennese, in their concern with themselves and their own image, develop what in Kraus's works would take on the significance of an aesthetic pattern and assert that their own city is an image of the way the world is, but that they perform this imaginative and artistic act in the context of reality and not in that of art; they are unable or unwilling to see that art is different from life. Their "provincialism" cannot really be so called, because it is so self-conscious, and to overlook that self-consciousness is to run the risk of misunderstanding such writers as Kraus and Nestroy.

There are then two errors proceeding from the same misconception of the nature of art; Nestroy, as I shall try to show in the second part of the present article, is concerned with the illegal importing of art into reality, whilst Kraus is in many ways concerned with the transformation of reality into art. For the confusion he blames the journalist:

> Er hat immer die größten Themen und unter seinen Händen kann die Ewigkeit aktuell werden; aber sie muß ihm auch ebenso leicht wieder veralten. Der Künstler gestaltet den Tag, die Stunde, die Minute. Sein Anlaß mag zeitlich und lokal noch so begrenzt und bedingt sein, sein Werk wächst umso grenzenloser und freier, je weiter es dem Anlaß entrückt wird. (. . .) Was vom Stoff lebt, stirbt vor dem Stoffe. Was in der Sprache lebt, lebt mit der Sprache.[1]

Kraus's restriction of his material to a large degree to Vienna and to the events reported in its newspapers may be seen as a deliberate artistic effort to avoid journalistic generalisations. Certainly he is prepared to ape the journalistic manner and take it to its logical conclusion in the complete confusion of the trivial and the important, the international and the local; as he does, for instance, in "Fahrende Sänger", when the news of universal suffrage is overshadowed by telegraphic reports of the antics of the Wiener Männergesangverein on their way to America. Instead of protesting, or giving his own account of the politics, he follows up the implications of this attitude by concentrating on the Männergesangverein and introducing politics only in the context of their gastronomic preferences: "die Kapitulation konservativer Schiffsköche".[2] By this, he implies the transposition of all events into the terms of the Männergesangverein's world—this is the only way in which politics can appear in it; to appreciate this, it helps if one has some idea of the "conventional image" of the Männergesangverein, although this is hardly essential and can be derived precisely from the linguistic formulation that Kraus gives of these transpositions. Nonetheless, the procedure argues familiarity with such an image most likely to be produced within the restricted frame of reference of Vienna.

Once again, it is the transposition, the pattern, that is important, and not the components, and in "Fahrende Sänger" Kraus often need do no more than quote verbatim a newspaper account of the voyage. For, even more important than the pattern is the perception of the pattern, especially if this can be produced by no more than an injunction to look closely, which implies that what one would take as merely contingent is in fact necessary and invites us to find the links. Kraus does this in the last of his polemics against Alfred Kerr, where he simply reprints Kerr's reply to him and adds:

> Es ist das Stärkste, was ich bisher gegen den Kerr unternommen habe.[3]

Pointless to object that it was written by Kerr; Kraus has claimed it, by the right of artistic perception and assertion, as a parody: this piece of writing is not merely by Kerr, it is an image of the way Kerr is.

Kraus is by no means always able to complete this process by means of simple suggestion. In the preface to *Die Letzten Tage der Menschheit* he is careful to explain why he has preserved the local details:

> Larven und Lemuren, Masken des tragischen Karnevals, haben lebende Namen, weil dies so sein muß und weil eben in dieser vom Zufall bedingten Zeitlichkeit nichts zufällig ist. Das gibt keinem das Recht, es für eine lokale Angelegenheit zu halten.[4]

What seems to be contingent, is in fact necessary; two flattering unctions are available in such cases of guilt—either accusations are too general, and there is no specific blame to be apportioned, or they are too specific to be generally applicable.

Strangely enough, these two possible excuses correspond to two ways of misunderstanding what Kraus is trying to do in *Die Letzten Tage der Menschheit*; one way involves the predictable confusion of the aesthetic pattern and its components, so that everything acquires merely local relevance and is hence made relative, whilst the second way assumes that Kraus is employing local material in the second of the three modes we defined, that is to say, that his message can be stated in abstract terms and is readily separable from the local frame of reference which he has chosen to present it. In either case, such misunderstandings proceed from a reluctance to use the imagination, a "failure to experience", of which Kraus accuses his contemporaries:

> Denn über alle Schmach des Krieges geht die der Menschen, von ihm nichts mehr wissen zu wollen, indem sie zwar ertragen, daß er ist, aber nicht, daß er war.[5]

Kraus explains his purpose and his methods more fully in the work itself (Act V, Scene 54):

> Hätte man die Stimme dieses Zeitalters in einem Phonographen aufbewahrt, so hätte die äußere Wahrheit die innere Lügen gestraft und das Ohr diese und jene nicht wiedererkannt. So macht die Zeit das Wesen unkenntlich, und würde dem größten Verbrechen, das je unter der Sonne, unter den Sternen begangen war, Amnestie gewähren. Ich habe das Wesen gerettet und mein Ohr hat den Schall der Taten, mein Auge die Gebärde der Reden entdeckt, und meine Stimme hat, wo sie nur wiederholte, so zitiert, daß der Grundton festgehalten blieb für alle Zeiten. (. . .) Ich habe die Tragödie, die in die Szenen der zerfallenden Menschheit zerfällt, auf mich genommen, damit sie der Geist höre, der sich der Opfer erbarmt, und hätte er selbst für alle Zukunft der Verbindung mit einem Menschenohr entsagt.[6]

The 'Wesen' which Kraus has preserved is evidently the aesthetic pattern of the work itself, the real occurrences transformed into images and hence no longer subject to the sort of practical considerations which would relativise them. The transposition into different sensory modes, "den Schall der Taten", "die Gebärde der Reden", indicates that the speeches and deeds are to be apprehended in some way which gives them a shape and an identity different from that which they would normally have in practical terms in their own contexts. It is clear from the end of the passage quoted that Kraus regards this transformation of the facts as the only possible form of expiation; practical reparations would be insufficient, and it seems only just, in Kraus's terms, that the war should finally be apprehended on the level of imagination, the lack of which he blamed for its inception and continuance.

Let us cite two examples of this transformation, one specific in time, to illustrate the general point, the other unashamedly local in origin. In Act IV, Scene 45 Graf Dohna-Schlodien is interviewed by twelve reporters about his sinking, as a U-boat captain, of a ship containing twelve hundred horses. Among the visions in Act V, Scene 55 the horses reappear and, like the figures in one of Goethe's later dramas, one of the "Festspiele", such as *Pandora* which Kraus revered so highly, or the pageant-like passages of *Faust II*, they utter their verses of revenge:

> Oh Dohna, wir suchen dich auf im Traum.
> Uns wollte der Platz nimmer taugen.
> Wir hatten kein Licht, zuviel Wasser hat Raum
> In zweimal zwölfhundert Augen.

> *Graf Dohna umgeben von zwölf Vertretern der Presse. Plötzlich stehen statt ihrer zwölf Pferde da. Sie dringen auf ihn ein und töten ihn.*[7]

In the horses' reappearance the transformation is made manifest which had been prepared for in the earlier scene; insofar as the interview takes place within the artistic context of *Die Letzten Tage der Menschheit* we can regard the sinking of the shipload of horses as already being an image. The act itself is one of brutal futility; in Kraus's hands it becomes an image of that brutal futility, and not a mere example or instance, so that the dead horses, rescued into the realm of the imagination, can take their revenge.

The second example concerns a specific allusion to something of which only a Viennese could realise the full significance. In his attack on Franz Josef in Act IV, Scene 29 the Nörgler speaks of:

> . . . die angestammte Schlamperei, die das Justament zum fundamentum regnorum erkoren hatte . . .

For full comprehension we require certain pieces of information; one of these would be the full force of "justament" in the Viennese dialect (we can derive Franz Josef's habitual use of the phrase from other places in the text); another would be the fact that the motto on the inner side of the Burgtor, the gate leading from the Hofburg, the Imperial Palace, to the Ring, reads "justitia fundamentum regnorum". It would be possible here to explain the image, without explaining it away into its component parts, although this would result in oversimplification; thus: the "justitia" that appears externally proclaimed as the basis of the Austrian monarchy is, in fact, private caprice, the image for which happens to be the word "justament". Kraus is, then, taking two elements from his restricted Viennese frame of reference and bringing them into a relationship with one another; the motto, taken as an image of the Habsburg monarchy and its public face, and the word, taken as an image of Franz Josef's behaviour. Kraus's conflation of the two is an image of their relationship, and whilst this image is dependent upon and only possible within this specific frame of reference, this restriction surely cannot render it invalid, any more than the fact that a play upon words is only possible in one language can render invalid an insight based on that play on words; if the insight is worth it, one learns the language.

We have spoken repeatedly of a restricted frame of reference and we suggested at the beginning that the Viennese were very conscious of their own and of the relationships obtaining within it; witness such long-lived publications as the *Eipeldauer Briefe* and *Hans Jörgel*, both purporting to give a "country cousin's" account of life in the Big City, as well as the transposition of all dramatic plots, serious or not, into Viennese terms: *Othellerl, der Mohr von Wien*, *Fiesko, der Salamikrämer*, *Die Frau Ahndl* (Grillparzer's *Ahnfrau*), and even Werther, who, in Kringsteiner's play, is saved from a watery grave in the Donaukanal by one of the poodles being trained in retrieving there. In *Robert der Teuxel*, his parody of Meyerbeer's grand opera, *Robert le Diable*, Nestroy performs a similar transposition, but sheds an ironic light on the whole procedure. On the one hand, there is the self-satisfied provincialism of Reimboderl, who is so proud of coming from Stadl Enzersdorf, an utterly insignificant village. On the other hand, Nestroy selects, as the counterpart to the ruined abbey, haunted by ghostly nuns, of the French original, a "Zauberweinkeller" near Gumpoldskirchen (most famous of the wine villages) staffed by spirits disguised as "fesche Kellnerinnen", and here we see the effects of the pattern so readily derived from a restricted frame of reference being applied as rules for behaviour: one of the spirits almost gives the game away by her strange behaviour in rejecting Robert's caress (Act III, Scene 8):

LENERL: Zurück! Nicht anrühren!
ROBERT (*betroffen*): Was? Und du nennst dich Kellnerin?[8]

As with Kraus, one must not take things at face value and see this passage as a sad comment on the nature of waitresses in Vienna. What matters is not whether Robert's expectations are justified, but the nature of them combined with the fact that he has them. The choice of a "Zauberweinkeller" suggests the sort of image the Viennese have of themselves which makes such a setting available to the dramatist for transposition, which must be easily recognisable as such.

Thus Nestroy is not operating with the reality of Vienna, but with the image of that reality which the Viennese themselves accept; and he employs it in such a way as to make clear the process by which the Viennese produce what might be an aesthetic pattern, but then proceed to treat it as if it were part of reality. The effect is of compiling recipes for events and then acting them out. What was contingent in reality is regarded as necessary in the formula; thus, in *Freiheit in Krähwinkel*, where the Viennese Revolution is taken as the model for a planned insurrection, it is necessary for young women to dress up as students, since you cannot have a proper revolution without them. A "proper revolution" obviously also needs the stock-figures which Ultra, the hero, impersonates by means of various disguises: a Liguorian monk (to be expelled), a Russian prince (to be feared), Metternich and a worker. Ultra's miniaturised account of the revolution points to the existence of a formula, an image for revolutions to which Krähwinkel must conform (I, 8):

> Alle Revolutionselemente, alles Menschheitsempörende, was sie wo anders in großem haben, das haben wir Krähwinkler in kleinem. Wir haben ein absolutes Tyrannerl, wir haben ein unverantwortliches Ministeriumerl, ein Bureaukratieerl, ein Zensurerl, Staatsschulderln, weit über unsere Kräfterln, also müssen wir auch ein Revolutionerl und durchs Revolutionerl ein Konstitutionerl und endlich a Freiheiterl krieg'n.[9]

This recipe has some of the characteristics of the aesthetic pattern, in that it seems to be separated from its context; however, the way that it is then immediately applied in the real world necessarily gives rise to contradictions, since the application occurs without regard to context or to the significance of the individual components, which has obviously been restored to them with their return to the real world.

Häuptling Abendwind, which is set on a cannibal island, has in the two cannibal chiefs characters of astounding provincialism whose attitudes and phraseology seem very Viennese. They open Scene 7 with the ritual greeting, performed, as is evident from the final comments, as a ritual:

> ABENDWIND: Mich g'freut's, daß Sie mir die Ehr' geben.
> BIBERHAHN: Bitte, die Ehre is meinerseits.
> ABENDWIND: Und wie geht's Ihnen denn immer?
> BIBERHAHN: Dank' für die Nachfrag', und Ihnen?
> ABENDWIND: Na, es muß schon gleich gut sein, bis es wieder besser wird.
> BIBERHAHN (*mit stolzem Selbstgefühl, beiseite*): Jetzt sollten uns die Zivilisierten hören.
> ABENDWIND (*beiseite*): Gibt es einen gebildeteren Diskurs!? Ah, wir Wilde haben schon auch unsere Kultur.[10]

Conformity with an image by no means guarantees the presence of those things which the image is supposed to represent. Excessive concern with the image encourages neglect of the realities. Thus it is that later in this same scene, having dismissed politics and contemplated a wholesale rejection of the modern world (Biberhahn says: "Kultur, Fortschritt, Zivilisation, alles batz' ich aus"), the two Viennese cannibal chiefs celebrate their image of themselves:

ABENDWIND: Mein Gott, man will ja eh nix, als daß man seine paar Bananen und sein Stückel G'fangenen in Ruh' verzehren kann.
BIBERHAHN: Freilich, wir sind ja gemütliche Leut'.
ABENDWIND: Recht rare primitive Kerle!
BEIDE (*zugleich, aber jeder beiseite*): Nur dann und wann fressen wir einer dem anderen die Gattin weg.[11]

Whilst it is arguable that such passages only have their full effect if we are already familiar with the "ready-made" nature of the platitudes exposed in them, it cannot be denied that these passages show up very accurately the discrepancy between image and reality.

Bound up with this idea of conforming to one's image is the question of "Selbstinszenierung", of merely acting a part, which is certainly not absent from Nestroy's plays. Titus Feuerfuchs, in *Der Talisman* (Act II, Scene 27), condemned to a tragic exit after his deception has been exposed, knows the right line to correspond to his situation:

Das ist Ottokars Glück und Ende! (*Geht langsam mit gesenktem Haupte zur Mitte ab.*)[12]

He also seems to know the right theatrical manner. His error lies in employing the image in a real situation. Being unaware of this Viennese trait (and in self-defence, I should like to plead that it is a qualitative and not quantitative matter and, like images, not strictly verifiable) one might have trouble in comprehending such passages. The same is true of Nestroy's use of stock jokes, such as the ones about bankruptcy; familiarity with the restricted frame of reference leads one to grasp more quickly that Weinberl's advice when possessed of insufficient finances for the restaurant bill in *Einen Jux will er sich machen*, Act II, Scene 16:

. . . Krida ist da, also verschwinden—das kommt im Merkantilischen häufig vor![13]

is not a comment on Viennese reality, but on the Viennese image of that reality. Modern adaptors of Nestroy often fall into the same trap and insert the wrong sort of topical allusion, one that is merely topical and does not have the appropriate position within the restricted frame of reference.

After all, the Viennese habit of claiming that their city is an image of the way the world is lies at the root of much of Nestroy, even when he employs it ironically, as in the famous "Kometenlied" in *Lumpazivagabundus* (Act III, Scene 8), where, in the second stanza, disaster is prophesied because the Viennese vices of drunkenness and milk-watering have reached the heavens:

Und der Mond geht auf so rot, auf Ehr',
Nicht anderster, als wann er b'soffen wär'.
Die Millichstraßen, die verliert ihr'n Glanz,
Die Milliweiber ob'n verpantschen s' ganz.[14]

As we saw with the Kraus example of the Burgtor motto, it is not the components, but the pattern and the relationship which are important.

As we have seen, both Kraus and Nestroy take the Viennese and their image of themselves and their habit of turning things (including themselves and their city) into images, and turn the whole into an image. Such an enterprise is only possible where the frame of reference is restricted, so that one can readily become aware of the relationships within it which are implied by asserting that it is an image of the way the world is.

The general points made in the present article may be of some use when considering other works which, because of their exclusive preoccupation with the details of unfamiliar areas, may be regarded as "provincial" and of merely local interest. The action of Bobrowski's *Levins Mühle*, for example, is only possible in the peculiar conditions of German Poland, with its complex religious and national rivalries; Bobrowski does not avoid charges of provincialism by showing up the timeless aspects; instead he introduces paragraphs that speculate on the transposition of the story into Latvian or Lithuanian areas, and how details such as names and titles would need to be altered to keep the same relationships between different races in different positions of authority. He has taken the Polish and Baltic area of German settlement as his image of the way the world is; and, indeed, in his second novel, *Litauische Claviere*, he not only does the same, but introduces characters who are attempting to write an opera on a Lithuanian theme and hence are in his own position, trying to make an image out of a restricted frame of reference, without reducing it to a set of generalised abstractions resting on too narrow a base.

Perhaps, though, there is something peculiarly Austrian in this readiness to see the microcosm as an image of the macrocosm. This is, after all, one way of explaining Stifter's continual presentation of landscape as image and the way he explores and elucidates natural relationships within his restricted frame of reference (for example, the mountain in *Bergkristall*, with all its differing functions) and makes them, without abstraction, into universal laws; he achieves his version of a resurrection myth by simple topographical statement.

Yet the whole procedure has a sense of irony about it; in Herzmanovsky-Orlando's *Der Gaulschreck im Rosennetz*, a skilful and self-indulgent exercise in Viennoiserie, there is a sense that the protagonist's tragic fate (he shoots himself after being surprised with a very young prostitute, whom he has hired in order to get one of her milk teeth to complete a garland of milk teeth he is preparing for the Emperor's jubilee) is directly brought about by the fact that this bizarre and complex invented world is, for him, the only one. The Viennese adoption of an artistic procedure as a way of life, with all the self-consciousness that implies, cannot help having theatrical overtones, so that Hebbel was accurate in the image he employed:

> Dies Österreich ist eine kleine Welt,
> In der die große ihre Probe hält.[15]

M. A. ROGERS

Southampton

NOTES

[1] "Heine und die Folgen", Karl Kraus, *Werke*, VIII (Munich, 1960), 195.

[2] "Fahrende Sänger", Karl Kraus, *Werke*, XII (Munich, 1964), 112.

[3] Karl Kraus, *Werke*, VI (Munich, 1958), 214.

[4] Karl Kraus, *Werke*, V (Munich, 1957), 9.

[5] Ibid., p. 10.

[6] Ibid., p. 681.

[7] Ibid., p. 720.

[8] Johann Nestroy, *Gesammelte Werke* [= *GW*], ed. O. Rommel (Vienna, 1948-49), II, 52.

[9] *GW* V, 75.

[10] *GW* VI, 505.

[11] *GW* VI, 507.

[12] *GW* III, 478.

[13] *GW* III, 657.

[14] *GW* I, 632.

[15] "Prolog zur festlichen Feier des Verfassungs-Tages", lines 97-8, Hebbel, *Werke*, III, ed. G. Fricke, W. Keller and K. Pörnbacher (Munich, 1965), 136.

VIII

ÖDÖN VON HORVÁTH:
KASIMIR UND KAROLINE

Horváth's main credential as an Austrian writer, in the old Danube-monarchy sense, is his refusal to lay claim to any national identity save that of the (south) German language. Born in 1901, the son of a Hungarian petty aristocrat in the Diplomatic Service, in the Croatian sector of the Italian enclave of Fiume (Rijeka), he was the child of a typical Civil Service family of the Austro-Hungarian Empire. The place of his birth was entirely fortuitous: his childhood and adolescence were spent in Belgrade, Budapest, Pressburg (Bratislava), Vienna and Munich. He regarded himself as fortunate to be free of any sentimental attachment to place or country. He took his *Matura* in Vienna, studied in Munich, and moved with his parents, when they retired, to Murnau in Upper Bavaria. In 1926 he set himself up in Berlin, the cultural capital of the inter-war period, but after 1934 Germany became too unhealthy for him and he settled in Henndorf near Salzburg. His flight from the Nazis was resumed in 1938. He was killed on 1 June in that year by a falling tree, during a freak storm in the Champs-Elysées. His *œuvre*, including seventeen plays, was produced almost exclusively during the decade before his bizarre death.

He called himself "eine typische österreichisch-ungarische Angelegenheit",[1] and his language comprises Hungarian-German, Bohemian, Austrian, Yiddish, Jewish-Viennese and Bavarian elements. But references to Austria are infrequent in his writings. In complete contrast to his friend Joseph Roth, Horváth did not mourn the end of Austria-Hungary. He was of the wrong generation to do so, and too busy recording the imprint of his own peculiar times.

In the years when he was trying to establish himself as a dramatist, it was natural that he should look, not to a somewhat exhausted Vienna, but to the Berlin of such playwrights as Bert Brecht, Arnolt Bronnen, Carl Sternheim, Georg Kaiser, Hauptmann, Sudermann, Toller, Johannes R. Becher, Carl Zuckmayer, as well as writers and journalists like Erich Kästner, Heinrich Mann and Alfred Döblin. His literary début was completed by 1929, when Ullstein added him to their stable of promising young writers, alongside Brecht and Zuckmayer. None of his plays received its première in Vienna until 1935, by which time he had already become a semi-exile and faced a diminishing choice of theatres in the German-speaking world able or willing to stage his work. Because of this dependence it was perhaps expedient in 1935 to write as he did in a letter to the Kleines Theater in der Praterstraße in Vienna *apropos* of a production of *Kasimir und Karoline* (first produced in 1932 in Leipzig): "Als ich vor einem halben Jahr von der erfolgreichen Aufnahme meines Stückes 'Kasimir und Karoline' in Wien erfuhr, habe ich mich sehr gefreut, denn ich habe es immer gehofft und geahnt, daß meine Stücke gerade in Wien Verständnis finden müßten."[2] Vienna's relationship to Horváth, and his to her, has however been somewhat uneven. There was a strong reaction particularly against his *Volksstück Geschichten aus dem Wiener Wald* (1930: Austrian première 1948) which was misinterpreted as a scurrilous attack on Viennese *mores*.[3] He has won gradual recognition in Austria in later years, although even in 1964 a Viennese critic felt justified in complaining, on the occasion of a production of *Kasimir und Karoline*, "die Wiener haben bis heute noch nicht erkannt, daß hier einer ihrer Größten am Werk war. Sie spielen ihn selten."[4] In this, Vienna was not very far behind Germany, but nonetheless it is significant that it was in Hamburg and not in Austria that Horváth's works were eventually collected for publication.

Whether or not Horváth himself had any residual sense of his place in the Viennese theatrical tradition, especially after his return to Austria in the 'thirties, it is certainly true that, from the beginning, critics have not been shy of attributing Austrian characteristics to him. It is with Austrian writers such as Raimund, Karl Kraus, Anzengruber and above all Nestroy that comparisons have most frequently been made, though Brecht is frequently mentioned in this context too, as are Büchner, Georg Grosz, Karl Valentin and Zuckmayer. The most significant compliment that Austria has paid to him has come from the "Grazer Genieschule" of the 1960s, and particularly Peter Handke, who acknowledges a far greater affinity with Horváth's "irre Sätze, die die Sprünge und Widersprüche des Bewußtseins zeigen" than with Brecht's "unwirkliche, aber doch ergreifende Weihnachtsmärchen".[5]

It is not difficult to explore the theme of Horváth's "Austrianness" in terms of generalisations. He can, for example, easily be numbered among the school of Austrian artists and thinkers who foresaw more clearly than most the approaching end of a civilization. The majority were Jews (Horváth regretted that Jewishness was not one of his qualifications!). Erich Heller draws up a list that starts with Karl Kraus and ends with Ludwig Wittgenstein, and hazards a suggestion that what they have in common is a recognition of the irreversible loss of human "substance" or "character", "nature" or "virtue" (in the Latin sense of *virtus*) or "being" ". . . in einer Zeit, die sich immer hemmungsloser der technischen Versklavung alles Natürlichen anheimgab . . ."[6] Although Horváth is not mentioned in the list of honour, there is no one to whom these words apply with greater force.

But in the serious pursuit of Horváth's relationship to the Austrian tradition, it is the Nestroy-parallel that looks most promising. Space is lacking here to carry out a full comparison, but the affinities are striking, especially in Horváth's later work, when, significantly, his abode and his centre of gravity had moved from Germany to Austria.[7] The very term *Volksstück* which Horváth chose to use for some of his earlier plays, including *Kasimir und Karoline*, has a Viennese flavour. There is much that Nestroy would recognise in Horváth's *Volksstücke*. Usually, as one would expect, such features are developed considerably beyond the prototype. The parodistically contrived "happy ending" of Nestroy's plays is adopted by Horváth in his three best-known *Volksstücke* (*Italienische Nacht, Geschichten aus dem Wiener Wald* and *Kasimir und Karoline*) but with devastating satirical effect, for in each case the apparent "all's well that ends well' outcome is actually the prelude to further disaster. Both Nestroy and Horváth—and this is perhaps the most obvious point of contact—attack the language of everyday life, holding up clichés and conventional assumptions against the light of "reality". Nestroy's coffee-house revolutionaries in *Freiheit in Krähwinkel*, set in 1848, who convince themselves by their own rhetoric of the proximity of the Revolution, are the ancestors of the Social Democrats in Horváth's *Italienische Nacht* (set in a typical Krähwinkel, based on Murnau) who hold the Nazis at bay from their *Stammtisch* with the empty jargon of shop-soiled Marxism:

> STADTRAT *mit den Karten in der Hand*: Von einer akuten Bedrohung der demokratischen Republik kann natürlich keineswegs gesprochen werden. Schon weil es der Reaktion an einem ideologischen Unterbau mangelt. (*Werke*, Vol. 1, Erstes Bild, p. 103)

In both plays the authors expose the emptiness of slogans used on *both* sides, that of enlightenment as well as that of reaction. The difference is that where Nestroy shapes everything to the *point* of his satire, Horváth declines to bring out the point. The audience is required to do the work of recognising it, which is to say of recognising themselves.

But it is important to emphasize that there is much that Nestroy would have found strange in Horváth's *Volksstücke*: not merely their social and political concern (his own political commitment was as powerful, though stifled by the savage censorship of his day) but the apparent shapelessness, the absence of a comic plot with its mistaken identities and recognition-scenes—the stock-in-trade of the old Viennese *Volksstück*—the lack of witty aphorisms, word-play and neatly-contrived jokes, and of a clear-cut moral.

In his last years Horváth developed—some might say declined—from a modern Nestroy to a Nestroy-epigone. The comedies had always been "regressive", compared to the *Volksstücke*. *Zur schönen Aussicht* (1927) contains a good deal of traditional material—not of course confined to Viennese comedy—such as punning, linguistic traps ("ADA: Ist das die Sehnsucht? KARL: Nein, das ist Durst." *Werke*, Vol. 3, p. 30), quick-fire burlesque jokes ("MULLER *nippt an seinem Glase*: Ich finde den Sekt recht ordentlich. Oder? MAX: Oder." p. 33) and arabesques ("STRASSER: . . . Ja wagst du zu leugnen, Weib, daß, während ich dir zu Füßen lag, du über mein Haupt hinweg und hinter meinem Rücken umeinandergebuhlt hast?!" p. 51). This play and *Rund um den Kongreß* (1929) share the social concerns of the *Volksstücke*, yet demonstrate how Horváth's comic talent dilutes the expression of social commitment. The more numerous comedies produced in Horváth's Austrian, or at least post-*Volksstück*, phase, such as *Hin und Her*, *Himmelwärts*, *Mit dem Kopf durch die Wand*, *Figaro läßt sich scheiden* and *Ein Dorf ohne Männer*, are not obviously committed in the way that the earlier plays were. After the Nazi takeover, Horváth seems to turn to resources he had never fully exploited before. If his "pure" comedy of these years is escapist—and the accusation has of course been made[8]—then who can censure him, any more than one can censure the exiled Stefan Zweig, among others, for turning in the 'thirties to the historical novel as relief from an oppressive present?

Hin und Her (1933), for example, is described as a *Posse*. Its theme, the stateless person shuttled to and fro in a no-man's-land between two countries, each of which refuses him entry, has tragic potential and autobiographical relevance. But the play is content to be an entertainment, in an almost timeless setting, complete with Nestroy-style music and songs composed especially for the occasion (this was the first time that Horváth had written lyrics for one of his plays). Reminiscent of the old *Volksstück* tradition are comic names (Schmugglitschinski), comic asides, inventive language ("Malefizrekognosziererei") and word-play.

Horváth's plays undoubtedly became more Austrian, more "baroque" in style, structure and sentiments from 1933 onwards. *Himmelwärts* (1934) even has more than a touch of the old *Zauberstück*—It is indeed called "ein Märchen"—with the action taking place on three stage levels, Heaven, Earth and Hell. The transparent moral is reminiscent of the Viennese *Besserungsstück* as produced by Gleich, Raimund, and the early Nestroy. For all the sparkling humour of *Himmelwärts*, there is a certain melancholy in this recreation of the genre, for the original *Besserungsstück* was a demonstration of an accepted truth in the Biedermeier age, the thesis of the virtue of moderation and of unquestioning acceptance of one's lot, and consequently "the real aim of the *Besserungsstück* was to present not so much a proof as an entertaining theatrical realization of that thesis—it was, in short, less a moralistic aim than an aesthetic one."[9] The same applies to Horváth's later comedies, the important difference being that the aesthetic supplants the ethical simply because the notion of generally accepted moral truths is now inconceivable. What is implicit in the "escapism" of the comedies is made explicit in such serious works as *Don Juan kommt aus dem Krieg* (a play of 1936) and *Ein Kind unserer Zeit* (novel, 1937), which share the theme of the search for an ideal which is almost categorically stated to be dead.

The comedies of the 'thirties show a comic talent as great as Nestroy's. This talent had been rigorously disciplined in the *Volksstücke* in order to achieve realism rather than comic point. The comedy of the *Volksstücke* is, for the most part, the inherent comedy of people trying to cover up their helplessness with a debased language, what Horváth called the *Bildungsjargon*, like a badly-cut, mass-produced coat that fits all and none. The only traditional definition of a *Volksstück* that would be appropriate to

Horváth's plays is a very loose one: "a play about ordinary people, for the entertainment and instruction of ordinary people". Many of Horváth's own remarks about the term are equally vague, as is his allusion to the traditional models he had in mind:

> Ich gebrauchte diese Bezeichnung "Volksstück" nicht willkürlich, d.h. nicht einfach deshalb, weil meine Stücke mehr oder minder bayerisch oder österreichisch betonte Dialektstücke sind, sondern weil mir so etwas ähnliches, wie die Fortsetzung des alten Volksstückes vorschwebte.—Des alten Volksstückes, das für uns junge Menschen mehr oder minder natürlich auch nur noch einen historischen Wert bedeutet, denn die Gestalten dieser Volksstücke, also die Träger der Handlung haben sich doch in den letzten zwei Jahrzehnten ganz unglaublich verändert. (*Werke*, Vol. 1, p. 11)

Some help is available from the *Gebrauchsanweisung* which was written specifically as an aid to the production of *Kasimir und Karoline*. It is one of Horváth's rare theoretical utterances, to which he felt compelled by the maltreatment his play had received at the hands of its producers. For an understanding of the term *Volksstück* as Horváth employs it, the main point in the *Gebrauchsanweisung* is his conception of the nature of the *Volk*. He wishes, he says, to revive the *Volksstück*, a kind of play "in dem Probleme auf eine möglichst volkstümliche Art behandelt und gestaltet werden", the basis of a theatre "das an die Instinkte und nicht an den Intellekt des Volkes appelliert" (*Werke*, Vol. 8, p. 662). But the *Volk* is not what it was. Germany, like every other modern state, consists almost entirely of petty bourgeois, *Kleinbürger*. This broad mass speaks a new language, divorced from its original dialects; Horváth's *Bildungsjargon*. It is the contemporary language of the half-educated, full of unassimilated scraps of knowledge and opinion, reflecting the decline of a culture and a moral code to a *Kitsch* collection of trivia. The more shaky the culture, the more likely people are to mouth self-deceptive moral platitudes.

Kasimir und Karoline, completed by December 1931, is the most representative of Horváth's *Volksstücke* because its subject-matter is nothing more nor less than this *Bildungsjargon*. Although it is not about politics like *Italienische Nacht*, *Kasimir und Karoline* is nonetheless highly relevant to politics, since man as a political animal is unfortunately dependent on the *Bildungsjargon*. By comparison with *Geschichten aus dem Wienerwald*, the plot is minimal, and there is less obvious dramatic material: the demonic aspects of everyday life are not so close to the surface (one thinks of the murder-by-neglect of the baby in *Geschichten*). There is no suicide, as in *Glaube Liebe Hoffnung*, a play which is moreover provided with the clear-cut "kleine Paragraphen" theme—remarkably close to that of Zuckmayer's *Der Hauptmann von Köpenick*—of the citizen caught up in the inexorable machinery of the law because of some petty infringement. *Kasimir und Karoline* is a "pure" form of the *Volksstück*, whose evidence on the state of contemporary consciousness is presented without the support of an obvious thematic framework, and is therefore all the more disturbing for the audience. The play certainly does nothing to give the lie to Horváth's claim in the *Gebrauchsanweisung* that the mere interaction of two personalities is sufficient for the creation of drama.

The action of the play is based on nothing more rigid than a casual crossing of paths at the *Oktoberfest* in Munich. It is the height of the Depression. Kasimir has just been dismissed from his job as a chauffeur, while Karoline's salary as a typist is a pittance; but Karoline's parents, with whom she lives, are economically cushioned by that most coveted of privileges, a civil servant's pension, and this discrepancy in the economic situations of the two lovers is the cause of a friction which quickly—they hardly know how—splits them apart, to drift around the vast *Oktoberwiese* in search of new pleasures, new partners, or even each other.

The play consists of many short scenes, and its structural backbone is provided by seven separate encounters between the two main figures as they constantly collide and part, like atoms in a void. The pleasure-ground setting is a fertile one. In seeking diversion, Horváth's characters come face to face with reality. The democracy of the *Oktoberfest* is illusory. Though all are joined in an off-duty, private purpose, and supposedly on an equal footing in the freemasonry of pleasure, in fact the class distinctions emerge more clearly than ever they do in ordinary "public" life. As Rauch, the department-store owner, remarks to his North German friend Speer, the judge, "Da sitzt doch noch der Dienstmann neben dem Geheimrat, der Kaufmann neben dem Gewerbetreibenden, der Minister neben dem Arbeiter—so lob ich mir die Demokratie!" (Sc. 23)—but then both old gentlemen move off to buy themselves a chicken from a stall otherwise deserted "weil alles viel zu teuer ist". Their power to consume conspicuously appears more naked than it would in the ordinary round of their more discreet luxuries. Conversely, for most people at the *Oktoberfest*, the heightened quest for gratification that the fair represents only leads to a rather exaggerated form of the disappointment which is the common lot. With millions unemployed, there is an underlying insecurity which finally erupts into a violent free-for-all. As the busy *Sanitäter* subsequently remarks: "Die Leute sind halt alle nervös und vertragen nichts mehr" (Sc. 103).

Karoline is at the centre of the action as, after an unaccustomed drink, she falls into the role of the typical *Wiesenbraut*, allowing herself the illusion that she is making rapid progress up the social ladder through her conquests, first of Schürzinger, a tailor's cutter, and then of his boss, Rauch. When the latter collects the wages of sin in the form of a heart attack, she tries to return to her first partner, Kasimir. But he, after an increasingly drunken evening spent railing against Karoline and the state of the world, has turned to Erna, whose "fiancé", Merkl Franz, has just been arrested for stealing from vehicles in the car park. Karoline takes up with Schürzinger again, and the two new couples are all set to provide a "happy ending", in accordance with the cynical motto with which Horváth prefaced the play: "Und die Liebe höret nimmer auf." "Love" never ends; only the names change.

The chief mechanism operating in the play, at first sight, seems to be a brutal automatism. One of the clearest examples is the scene in which Kasimir learns the facts of economic life at first hand. He has persuaded Elli, a girl of dubious morals, to sit in his lap, with the promise of a glass of beer; but the discovery that he has no money left is followed by some rapid automatic developments:

> KASIMIR *kramt in seinen Taschen*: Zahlen bitte, zahlen bitte—ja Herrgottsackelzement, hab ich denn jetzt da schon das ganze Geld weg—*Kellnerin nimmt die Maß wieder mit.*
> *Elli erhebt sich.* (Sc. 67)

Schürzinger extrapolates the logic of this situation and applies it to Kasimir and Karoline when he suggests to the latter: ". . . Nehmen wir an, Sie lieben einen Mann. Und nehmen wir weiter an, dieser Mann wird nun arbeitslos. Dann läßt die Liebe nach, und zwar automatisch" (Sc. 4).

The play is on one level a demonstration of the truth of Schürzinger's theory (irrespective of the fact that it is deployed by him tactically rather than with a genuine desire to enlighten Karoline). The cash-nexus creates a kind of tropism which leads Karoline inexorably in the direction of money and—perhaps even more important—the hope of security. A relationship with Rauch, based on money, promises her a satisfyingly effortless and un-complex life. She indulges in a kind of wilful simplification which is later echoed by Kasimir, the ex-chauffeur, in a speech reminiscent of a Nestroy *Metier-Lied*:

> KASIMIR: So ein Weib ist ein Auto, bei dem nichts richtig funktioniert —immer gehört es repariert. Das Benzin ist das Blut und der Magnet das Herz—und wenn der Funke zu schwach ist, entsteht eine Fehl-zündung—und wenn zuviel Öl drin ist, dann raucht er und stinkt er —. (Sc. 110)

Kasimir chooses to see the female as functional and simple, avoiding all the regrettable psychological realities and the complex demands made by each side in a relationship The simplification inherent in this "mechanical bride" approach suggests the unconscious fears of Kasimir. It transfers the mal-function of his love-affair to the machine (i.e. to Karoline), which is said to be unreliable, and thus covers up the impotence of the male in a world where loss of work equals loss of potency. This equation in its turn is a simplification, and one which is brutally applied to Kasimir by his would-be pick-ups Elli and Maria, to whom he had pretended that he owned a car:

> MARIA: Und so was möchte einen Kompressor haben? Ich hab es dir ja gleich gesagt, daß so etwas im besten Falle ein Fahrrad hat. Auf Abzahlung
> KASIMIR *zu Elli*: Komm, geh her—
> ELLI *winkt*: Grüß dich Gott, Herr Kompressor—*Ab mit Maria.* (Sc. 67)

Automatism is a part of the everyday experience of the characters in the play, a deformation of their lives. Certain assumptions are automatic to them, so that when a crisis occurs they tend to give way fatalistically to such preconceptions as: a mere chauffeur has no right to expect a salaried office-worker to marry him; a cutter is better than a chauffeur; a girl whose father is a *Beamter* with a pension should marry another pensionable *Beamter*, and so on.[10] And yet it would be too great a reduction simply to say that the play is only a study of the effects of social pressure on certain preconditioned subjects. The real concern of the play is the inadequacy of modern man to handle the crisis situation. Where, in less difficult times, he would have muddled through with his ignorance and his ill-formed assumptions, the Depression forces him into a confrontation with polarities, just as politics tend to become polarized and extreme in a crisis. The language he uses is the medium of his inadequacy, his confusion, and his attempts to overcome his difficulties. Above all, it is the self-defeating medium through which he tries to assert his individual identity.

Horváth demanded that his *Volksstücke* should be acted not in dialect, but in a *Hochdeutsch* which revealed the obsolete dialect not too far below the surface. Such an overlaying of native idiom by an acquired language expresses uncertainty and insecurity on the part of the speaker, even inadequate control of the thinking process itself. Dialogue often proceeds by means of "irre Sätze" (to use Handke's phrase) with a logic all of their own, such as Kasimir's "Wir sind alle nur Menschen! Besonders heute!" (Sc. 67); or Erna's pronouncement, opening up curious perspectives: "Wenn ich ein Mann wär, dann tät ich keine Frau anrühren. Ich vertrag schon den Geruch nicht von einer Frau. Besonders im Winter" (Sc. 60). Karoline sums up the process involved in such formulations: "Ich denke ja gar nichts, ich sage es ja nur" (Sc. 52). Language runs on in neutral because the mind itself is idling, reminding us of the injunction sometimes displayed in offices: "Before opening mouth, engage brain!" However, the uncertainty of their command of language is not consciously apparent to the characters themselves. The more they flounder, the more likely they are to use words that imply certainty and mastery of the situation (just as both Kasimir and Karoline create their respective simplified views of the opposite sex, out of confusion and insecurity). Words like "akkurat", "radikal", "eigentlich", "automatisch", "konstatieren", "genau", "bestimmt", "absolut" and "unberufen" abound in Horváth's dialogue. The show of strength invariably means weakness. The most extreme case is that of Merkl Franz, a would-be *Kraftmensch* who claims to be the master of his fate, and linguistically demonstrates his mastery by means of such global *Bildungsjargon* terms as "Weltsituation": "In einer derartigen Weltsituation muß man es eben derartig machen, wie zum Beispiel ein gewisser Merkl Franz" (Sc. 68). In reality he is a tubercular petty thief unlikely to survive the rigours of the gaol sentence he will inevitably receive.

Everywhere characters are looking for some way, however absurd, of giving order to life and relieving their uneasiness, like Erna's: "Wissens, wenns mir schlecht geht, dann denk ich mir immer, was ist ein Mensch neben einem Stern. Und das gibt mir dann wieder einen Halt" (Sc. 12). Many of the speeches ostensibly intended to persuade others of something are actually attempts at self-persuasion, usually calling upon some ready-packaged *Bildungsjargon* formula: "KAROLINE Oh nein! Wenn es dem Manne schlecht geht, dann hängt das wertvolle Weib nur noch intensiver an ihm—könnt ich mir schon vorstellen" (Sc. 4). The hesitation couched in more natural speech tagged on to the end of the *Hochdeutsch* sentence, and inviting contradiction, indicates her real lack of conviction and direction. The linguistic duels of Kasimir and Karoline consists of arguments directed towards themselves as much as to each other, by which they seek to dress up as rational principle what is in fact self-indulgence. With each utterance they become more convinced of the rightness of their own "views", by a process that has been called "ein 'psycho-akustischer' Rückkoppelungsmechanismus".[11] The *Bildungsjargon* leads almost automatically to this result, since its very employment is a means of distancing oneself from the conversational partner, a "put-down", as the modern colloquialism has it. At crucial moments Kasimir cannot resist conducting his affair with Karoline as though it were an official interrogation, using proper bureaucratic *Hochdeutsch* which painstakingly misses the point of the hitch in their relationship. As Walder points out,[12] the *Bildungsjargon* is not just an automatic response, but is irresistibly attractive, raising the individual—as he thinks—out of the despised mass on to a higher, educated plane, to an individuality that seems to guarantee a private and personal consciousness. This individual consciousness, however, is precisely what he does *not* have; and at some level he has a nagging awareness that he does not have it.

Horváth's favourite stage-direction, *Stille*, brings out the shortfall between the pretensions of his characters and their deeper suspicion, which they could never formulate, that they *are* merely pretensions. Horváth drew special attention in his *Gebrauchsanweisung* to the significance of silences in his dialogue, as moments when the conscious mind struggles with the unconscious (*Werke*, Vol. 8, p. 664) and went so far as to declare this the mainspring of all his dramatic works: "Das dramatische Grundmotiv aller meiner Stücke ist der ewige Kampf zwischen Bewußtsein und Unterbewußtsein" (*Werke*, Vol. 8, p. 659). In other terms, it is the struggle between the public world and the private. The chief power of the *Bildungsjargon* is its independent and public nature, its tendency to take over the speaker. The language is a collective product, and belongs to no one individual to command or dispose of according to his will. Like Karl Kraus, Horváth puts language at the centre of the crisis of his time. He was in the habit of re-distributing speeches among characters from one version to the next, a clear indication of the loss of individuality, and of the collective nature of the language. Where the language offers the temptation of inter-changeable and impersonal units of speech, political parties and sexual partners too can become interchangeable units.

This is no more what most of the characters actually want or believe to be the case than is their domination by the arbitrary nature of the *Bildungsjargon*. The point is underlined by a contrast that is more apparent than real. On the one hand we have the brutality of Merkl Franz in stating this principle of interchangeability—"Weiber gibts wie Mist" (Sc. 18); and on the other hand Kasimir's transparent self-deception when, after first carefully enquiring whether Erna is healthy, he throws a threadbare cover of romantic predestination over their arbitrary coupling with the phrase "Ich glaub, wir sind zwei verwandte Naturen." Erna rises to the occasion with a stilted variation on Goethe's "Warum gabst du uns die tiefen Blicke": "Mir ist es auch, als täten wir uns schon lange kennen" (Sc. 112). Indeed they *have* known each other "schon lange", in so far as they are not indi-viduals but interchangeable units. What it amounts to is no more than that "Weiber (Männer) gibts wie Mist".

The play is scattered with partial insights, political or otherwise, adding a tantalizing extra dimension. Typically these occur, for example, when a personal set-back has been suffered, as in Kasimir's monologue in Sc. 62 (the paradigm for this process is the hero of Horváth's last novel, *Ein Kind unserer Zeit*, a proto-Fascist who only gains political insight when he is no longer fit to serve in his beloved Army). Such insights are nullified by being based on bad faith or lack of self-awareness; they are often produced to fit the characters' tactics of the moment. Franz justifies his anti-social life of crime as a one-man anti-capitalist campaign of stealing from "hoch-kapitalistische Limousinen" belonging to "lauter Steuerhinterzieher" (Sc. 86). It would be out of character for Kasimir to turn to crime, and he rejects this course with an apparent insight, in reality a specimen of *Bildungsjargon* derived ultimately from Marx: "so private Aktionen haben keinen Sinn" (Sc. 68). It is a pseudo-insight. (The momentary tactical purpose of this remark of Kasimir's is revealed by a later variation on it after Merkl Franz's arrest, when Kasimir reiterates "Ich habe es immer gesagt, daß so *kriminelle* Aktionen keinen Sinn haben." Sc. 112). If an insight appears to hit the nail on the head, as likely as not the accuracy results from an accidental overlap of sentiment and situation. Erna plays upon her revolutionary connexion, a brother shot in 1919, to attract Kasimir's sympathy, but her picture of the Revolution is pure, unpolitical *Kitsch*.

The "Dichte der Atmosphäre" for which Horváth has often been praised does not depend upon the dialogue alone, but is augmented by a rich acoustic and visual backdrop. Music, a standard constituent of the old *Volksstück*, is put to new uses. It enhances the discrepancies between the public and the private spheres which are implicit in the dialogue and are often marked by the stage direction *Stille*. Scene 102 is the sequel to the outbreak of general fighting in the fairground. It contains only a stage direction, yet speaks for itself: "*Nun intoniert das Orchester piano den Waltzer 'Bist du's lachendes Glück?' und aus der Sanitätsbaracke treten Oktoberfestbesucher mit verbundenen Köpfen und Gliedmaßen, benommen und humpelnd . . .*"

Throughout the play, Kasimir has refused to join in the singing of songs, collective clichés which blatantly contradict the reality of his own situation and provide a pseudo-unity for the other characters. But in the last scene he is induced to join with Erna in singing:

'Nur der Mensch hat alleinig
Einen einzigen Mai."

The irony is that the song signals the blighting of this "einziger Mai", as Kasimir's hope for a genuine and individual relationship dies, leaving nothing but easy and generalized sentiment. Its death was similarly signalled musically when a melody (the "Militärmarsch 1822 von Schubert") was at last played through "zu Ende" (Sc. 99), previous tunes having been arrested in mid-phrase.

As a counter-attraction for the visitors to the *Oktoberfest*, Horváth introduces that technical *Abnormität*, the Zeppelin, and links it with the earth-bound freaks in the side-show below. Like the Man with the Bulldog Head, Juanita the Gorilla Girl, the Fat Lady and the Siamese Twins, the Zeppelin is a distraction from real life and the Depression, providing the displacement activity of looking *up*, rather than down into the depths of misery. Like Brecht's pilot in *Der gute Mensch von Sezuan*, it embodies collective aspirations, where individual ones are unrealizable ("EIN LILIPUTANER Wenn man bedenkt, wie weit es wir Menschen schon gebracht haben—." Sc. 3). It is at the same time a symbol of Germany's renewal. As the play opens, all are significantly united, rich and poor, midget and normals, in admiring this patriotic achievement in its passage overhead. In Scene 45, where the Zeppelin returns, the freak-show audience streams outside to see it and the freaks themselves follow suit to view the marvels of progress, to the horror of the cryer, who is given a rich line of dialogue: "DER AUSRUFER Direktor! Die Krüppel sind wahnsinnig geworden! Sie möchten den Zeppelin sehen!"

The escape of the *Abnormitäten* is a threat to business as bad as Communism, since it threatens to destroy the symbiotic relationship of exploiter to exploited, as the director-midget says: "DER LILIPUTANER . . . Auf die Plätze! Was braucht ihr einen Zeppelin zu sehen—wenn man euch draußen sieht, sind wir pleite! Das ist ja Bolschewismus!" (Sc. 45). We have here a stage-within-a-stage technique which closely parallels the "boxes within boxes" structure of Peter Weiss's *Marat/Sade*. Ultimately, perhaps, we recognize the analogy of the freaks' literal captivity and our own unfreedom within the cage of economic and social conditions. The threat of their escape is, furthermore—like the threatened revolt of the insane inmates of Charenton in *Marat/Sade*—a threat to let loose the unconscious element in "normal" people and break down the artificial barrier between the aberration and what is presumed to be normal. The entire purpose of the *Oktoberfest* is precisely to erect a barrier between the pursuit of distraction (pleasure) and "normal" everyday life (suffering). The participants are thereby distracted, not to say alienated, from their own condition. (This distraction technique was, of course, commonly exploited by Nazi demagogues, through the creation of dramatic incident, novelty and diversion.) The freaks, in this light, are representative of the truly human condition, beyond nationalism or self-delusion. The very notion of "an English freak" or "a German freak" is absurd.[13] By virtue of their abnormality they shed all pretensions and are simply *human*. Conversely the "normal" characters, by implication, are hard-pressed to avoid moral deformity in some form or other, a deformity which the *Bildungsjargon* easily imposes upon them.

Here, perhaps, we arrive at the heart of *Kasimir und Karoline*, and of Horváth's *Volksstücke*. What redeems his heroes is their absurd but attractive insistence on nursing aspirations (they "want to see the Zeppelin") even though in practice it is difficult enough for them to achieve a minimum individual identity (they are not so different from Juanita the *Gorillamädchen*, who feebly asserts her dignity: "Also beschimpfen laß ich mich nicht! *Sie weint.*" Sc. 45). The aspirations are always confused. In Karoline's case, snobbery and sentimentality conflate "higher things" with social superiority. But even the possession of aspirations indicates that freedom is not entirely lost. That *Kleinbürgertum* has not entirely repressed the healthy *Volk* in Karoline is made clear when she produces a line straight from Nestroy:[14] "Geh redens doch nicht immer so geschwollen daher" (Sc. 24). Kasimir and Karoline do at least struggle, with pitifully few weapons at their command, to preserve their freedom, however illusory. What makes them the heroes of the play is the psychological effort they put into their struggle for self-realization. Kasimir's case is the more tragic, for he pours all his aspirations into one relationship, which is made to bear too great a load—sex, ambition, insecurity, and his confrontation with hard times.

By the end of the play, the vestigial independence of both Kasimir and Karoline has been betrayed; they have become resigned to membership of the common herd. Kasimir is as brutal to Karoline in his dismissal of her as Franz was to Erna. Karoline adopts the vulgar invective of the amateur prostitutes Elli and Maria. Ironically, she leaves the stage intoning Emile Coué's phrase "es geht immer besser, immer besser"—the formula of a 'twenties cult of *self*-improvement, ironic in view of the fact that she has now forfeited all claim to the possession of a "self".

Horváth's power is to show us both the sociology of her failure and Kasimir's,[15] and also the poetry of it, the "awareness of the living, intense moment in the waste of time, dead or gone" which, it has been said, *is* the poetic emotion.[16] The mood of the play is summed up in Horváth's description in later years: "eine Ballade der Arbeitslosigkeit".

St Andrews   A. F. BANCE

NOTES

¹ *Gesammelte Werke*, ed. Traugott Krischke and Dieter Hildebrandt, Frankfurt a.M., 1972, Vol. 1, p. 7. All quotations from Horváth's works are taken from this edition.

² *Ödön von Horváth, Leben und Werk in Dokumenten und Bildern*, ed. Traugott Krischke and Hans F. Prokop, Frankfurt a.M., 1972, p. 99.

³ See *Materialien zu Ödön von Horváths "Geschichten aus dem Wiener Wald"*, ed. Traugott Krischke, Frankfurt a.M., 1973, p. 136 *et passim*.

⁴ Otto F. Beer, "Schwarzes Oktoberfest", *Neues Österreich*, Vienna 27.11.1964, quoted in *Materialien zu Ödön von Horváths "Kasimir und Karoline"*, ed. Traugott Krischke, Frankfurt a.M., 1973, p. 180.

⁵ *Materialien zu Ödön von Horváth*, ed. Traugott Krischke, Frankfurt a.M., 1970, p. 180.

⁶ Erich Heller, "Karl Kraus und die Ethik der Sprache", *Austriaca*, ed. Winfried Kudszus and Hinrich C. Seeba, Tübingen, 1975, p. 313.

⁷ Little is known about Horváth's reading, and as far as Nestroy is concerned we must fall back on an isolated, albeit admiring, reference. See *Ödön von Horváth, Leben und Werk in Dokumenten und Bildern*, p. 137.

⁸ See Dieter Hildebrandt, *Ödön von Horváth in Selbstzeugnissen und Bilddokumenten*, Reinbek bei Hamburg, 1975, p. 88 *et passim*.

⁹ W. E. Yates, *Nestroy*, Cambridge, 1972, p. 23.

¹⁰ See Elisabeth Meier, *Sprachnot und Wirklichkeitszerfall*, Düsseldorf, 1972, p. 29.

¹¹ Martin Walder, *Die Uneigentlichkeit des Bewußtseins: zur Dramaturgie Ödön von Horváths*, Bonn, 1974, p. 43.

¹² Op. cit., p. 46.

¹³ Cf. Ulrich Becher, "Stammgast im Liliputanercafé", *Materialien zu Ödön von Horváth*, p. 91, who quotes Horváth as having remarked "Ich hab nie einen Liliputaner-nazi getroffen".

¹⁴ *Zu ebener Erde und erster Stock*, Act I, Sc. 3: "SALERL Geh, du redst wieder so geschwollen."

¹⁵ Horváth's observations on the society of Weimar Germany tally remarkably well with those of Siegfried Kracauer in his famous study *Die Angestellten* (Frankfurt a.M., 1930), which picks out *inter alia* the *Bildungsjargon* phenomenon, the search for diversion, the results of job-insecurity (e.g. the employers' influence extends even into employees' private lives: cf. Rauch's treatment of his employee Schürzinger in *Kasimir und Karoline*); rigid class demarcation between lower-middle and working classes; the "feudal" nature of industrial bosses who replace the lost power of the pre-War state; and cults such as that of auto-suggestion and "self-improvement" popularized by Émile Coué. For further discussion of this comparison, see my contribution "Horváth and Social Reportage" to the *Symposium on Ödön von Horváth* published by the Austrian Institute (London, 1977). See also for reference to Horváth's background Peter Branscombe's contribution "The Austrian Volksstück Tradition" to the same publication.

¹⁶ Kathleen Nott, *The Emperor's Clothes*, London, 1953, p. 214.

This collection of eight essays covers aspects of Austrian life and literature from the time of Joseph II at the end of the 18th century up to the end of the First Republic. The essays explore relatively unfamiliar territory (Friedel's *Eleonore*, Horváth's *Kasimir und Karoline*, the 19th-century *Feuilleton*), or examine neglected and misunderstood aspects of the work of some of Austria's greatest writers (Grillparzer and the Realist tradition, Stifter's use of leitmotifs, the relationship between Nestroy and Karl Kraus, a neglected Nestroy play), or analyse myth and reality in Vienna's cultural life in the first half of the 19th century. The authors of the articles include both established leading experts in their field, and younger scholars of great promise and originality.

The increasing interest shown in British and American universities in Austrian literature and cultural life, combined with the varied and interesting subject-matter and the liveliness and expertise of the contributors, should ensure a widespread favourable response to this new volume.